D1594826

CLEAN:
From Reggae to Recovery

---

a memoir

David Smeltz
with
Jennifer Coiley

The names and identifying details of some characters
in this book have been changed.

Copyright © 2014 by David Hall Smeltz

All rights reserved, including the right of reproduction
in whole or in part in any form.

Cover photo and book design by Coy Lee Media
Text set in Minion

Manufactured in the United States of America

ISBN-10: 0-6922108-9-X
ISBN-13: 978-0-692-21089-5

Dedication

To my mother Inez Smeltz
for her consistent example of unconditional
love and compassion that inspires me daily.

To Tyrone Saunders
my best friend and brother in recovery.

Acknowledgments

I would like to thank my daughters, Kelsey and Shelbey Smeltz,
for providing the initial incentive to surrender.

Thank you to Jennifer Coiley for her hard work and publishing skills
to make this book a reality. Many thanks to Laura Coiley Dietrich
for her suggestion and encouragement to write.

There are many that I would like to thank for their contributions.
The most important of all would be my sponsor and friend,
Ron Harris, who introduced me to a new way to live.

Many thanks to all I-Tal band members past and present:
Chris Dunmore, Dave Valentine, John Wagner,
Bob Caruso, Carlos Jones, Mike Wasson, and George Gordon.

Special thanks to Felicia Saunders, Joann Bell, Abena Johnson,
Meg Elliott, Pastor Rob Edmonds, Craig H.,
Listen To Learn, my Homegroup members, John Visnauskas,
all 12 step programs, Lenzell P., Lisa Jones, Ravelle N., Sandra Santora,
William and Audrie Hall, Allison Hall,
Orca House, and The Salvation Army P.A.S.S. program.

It is with extreme gratitude that I thank Clyde Chafer for his
September, 2011 *Journey* magazine article which
prompted this title and the courage to share my experience.

My most special thank you is for a God of my understanding
through which all things are possible.

**All proceeds from the sale of this book will benefit
Clean House, Inc., a 501(c)3 non profit organization.**

Although the world is full of suffering,
it is also full of overcoming it.

– Helen Keller

PROLOGUE

January 2001

AFTER RUNNING UP to my mother's bedroom one night with a hammer, sweating profusely, claiming someone was behind the wall in the basement, my mother told me I had to leave her house. She quickly locked her bedroom door, and I ran back down to the basement where I was staying. I began to tear holes in the ceiling, looking for crack rocks that I had stashed for the future.

When I left her house eventually, I stayed at various motels and hotels around Cleveland. I wanted to get as high as possible to forget about the pain I was causing everyone around me. There wasn't enough dope to help me forget. I had taken the savings book from my wife's purse that gave me access to the proceeds from selling our first home, approximately $14,000. I knew that would piss her off, and that's exactly what I wanted to do.

Settling into a room at the Travel Lodge in Lakewood, I pulled out a supply of crack and heroin. The manager was nice, so I bought him a package of cookies. Later that evening, I started ruminating over my wife and missing her. I wanted to tell her how much I loved her and see if we could work things out. I called early in the morning, and when she answered, I got scared and didn't speak.

"Dave, is that you?" she asked. I mumbled something a couple of times. "You're not supposed to be talking to me!"

I hung up quickly. My wife dialed *69, calling the motel back. She told the manager that I was harassing her, and she was calling the police. The manager returned my cookies and kicked me out. I called my mother from a payphone. She said the police were looking for me, and I should turn myself in, or go to a hospital to get help with my drug problem.

When I arrived at the ER of Huron Road Hospital, I told the staff that I was a heavy crack and heroin user and needed help. I was asked to supply a urine sample and I lay on a gurney, where they shot me up with something to relax me. I felt like everything was going to be okay. A few minutes later, a Cleveland Heights policeman entered.

"David Smeltz?" he asked to which I nodded. "We've been looking for you." He promptly handcuffed me.

At Cleveland Heights city jail, the contents of my pockets – $15, a lighter, car keys – were placed into a plastic bag. My mug shot was taken, making all of the officers laugh. They passed it around to other officers in the building for their amusement. I was ushered into a cell where I started to detox from the remaining heroin in my system. After laying down on a concrete slab they called a bed, I became anxious to leave.

I called an attorney. I waited, waited and waited even longer. My back began to ache and my nose started running. I felt weaker and my thoughts became cloudy. I was detoxing. All I could think about was the 15 dollars I had and what I was going to do with it when I was released. My attorney told me that my mother wanted me to go for a psychiatric evaluation immediately upon release. I agreed to it so I could get out sooner.

The time came for my release, and I was given my money and other property. All I saw was the money. I was released into my mother's custody, and she drove me back to Huron Road Hospital where I had left my car.

"David," she said with a sigh. "You really need to get some help. I'm worried about you."

All I knew at that moment was that I needed heroin. She dropped me off on the first floor of the parking garage, and I walked up to the second floor to my car. It was a cold day, so I prayed for my car to start. It did. I cruised down to the first floor, down the ramp and past my mother, who was waiting to follow me to the psych eval. As I passed her I saw an expression on her face that I will never forget: hopelessness, bewilderment and despair. For the first time, I realized that heroin meant more to me than the love of my mother.

I vowed to stay away from the home where my wife and daughters were living, and used our savings for hotel rooms, dope, cigarettes, and gas. My thoughts raced the more I smoked. I started missing my kids, my mother and even my wife. To find out what they were doing, I decided to look in the phone book for a private investigator and called him.

"My wife is cheating on me," I told him. "I need evidence."

He said he would start on the case for $500, and I should meet him at a gas station. I checked out of the motel and immediately withdrew a couple thousand dollars. On the way to meet the investigator in Akron, I picked up an eight ball of crack and about six bags of heroin. I checked into a Holiday Inn and paid extra for a game system in my room. I smoked a little then went to meet him.

The guy knew I was loaded.

"I didn't know the subject is in Cleveland," he said. "Gonna need more money." I gave him another $500 and my room number to the Holiday Inn. "I'll stake out your house, and let you know about any men she's meeting." Just what I wanted to hear!

"I'll wait at the motel for updates," I told him.

Two days passed without a word. On the third day I called him and asked him what was up.

He yelled at me: "Don't call me. I told you I'd call you!" He hung up. I made a couple of runs to Cleveland for more dope to hold me over. A few more days went by and I called again. "The house looks empty," he snapped and hung up.

I checked out of the motel and returned to the family home in Cleveland Heights. I drove past the house a few times with caution, as there was still a restraining order, and I didn't want to be arrested for stalking my wife. I noticed there were no tire tracks in the snow on the driveway. Each day I passed the house, I didn't see tracks. I parked on the street behind our house one day and went through our neighbors' backyard to the back of our house. I saw an empty box on the patio and no footprints. All of the shades were drawn as I slowly crept up to the back window and peered through the venetian blinds. All of the furniture in the living room was gone! A sick feeling formed in the pit of my stomach and I became anxious. I broke the window, and climbed into the house. Everything was gone. I went upstairs. Our king-sized bed was gone. My daughters' beds, gone. Their toys, gone. I went to the basement and found a daybed, a stereo console my grandmother had given me, a freezer from my mom, and an old color TV with the antenna broken off that I used to smoke crack. I sat on the daybed and cried.

PART I

CHAPTER ONE

1968

I HAD MY first drink sometime after leaving sixth grade at Ludlow Elementary School and entering Woodbury Junior High. At the time, I lived on Onaway Road in Shaker Heights, Ohio, with my grandparents and mother. I attended canteens (dances) at Plymouth Church nearby on Drexmore Road. The kids I hung out with went to Ludlow, and were drinking wine once in a while, so I decided to impress them one night at a canteen. I poured some Old Grand Dad bourbon from my grandfather's bar into two empty Dristan spray bottles. At appropriate moments, I would spray the contents into my mouth. I wanted to smell like I had been drinking more than anything else. My friends were impressed, and I loved the feeling. It was rainy and cold that October day, but I didn't feel it after I killed the first spray bottle. We stayed at the church for an hour or so, and then escorted some girls across town to Menlo Road and Chagrin Boulevard. It was the best night of my life because I felt grownup and in control. I was talking to girls and drinking – pretty good for being fresh out of sixth grade! My Dristan experience progressed to taking one of my grandfather's Stroh's from the fridge. He and my grandmother, who grew up in a different time and place, didn't seem to mind. I didn't like the taste, but I did like the buzz. I felt in control and had an "I don't give a fuck" attitude. Not rude, just a sense of freedom.

Who is That Guy?

Before that, when I was about five or six, I looked through a box of photos one day. Some of the pictures had been cut in half, with my mother or grandmother remaining in the picture with a disembodied hand or arm. I asked once who the phantom hand/arm belonged to.

"Oh, that's Clayton," my grandmother said.

I didn't ask who Clayton was; just accepted it. Not long after, when I was playing with the kid next door whose family had recently moved in, we went into his kitchen where his mother greeted us. The kid started to introduce me to his mother when she cut him off.

"I know who he is," she snapped. Her tone of voice freaked me out. She pulled out an 8x10 glossy photo out of a drawer in the kitchen and stuck it in my face. "Do you know who this is?"

"Nope," I answered. She asked again, frowning. "No," I repeated.

She held the picture closer to my face and spewed, "That's Clayton!"

I didn't say anything; just wanted to leave the house. *Who the heck is this Clayton guy?*, I thought as I went home. My mother was standing at the kitchen sink when I came over to her.

"Who is Clayton?" I was very young, but to me it looked like she had shit her pants, as she had a really surprised look on her face.

"Who told you and what do you know about Clayton?" she asked sharply.

"The lady next door has a picture of him and was talking about him."

That was when it hit the fan.

Our relationship with the new neighbors changed at that moment. From then on, yelling matches back and forth ensued between my grandmother and the woman next door. An occasional dish had been thrown from either their house or ours, and shattered in the driveway between the houses. I remember my mother yelling at someone and slamming the front door one time. Prior to this, I never heard my mother raise her voice once; she was usually smiling and laid back. My grandmother, on the other hand, didn't play, as I experienced firsthand what she could do with the backside of a wooden hairbrush!

After a couple of weeks, things seemed to calm down.

I asked my mom again: "Who's Clayton?

"He's your father."

Inez and Clayton

I never thought about having a father until then. I had a grandfather and that had the word "father" in it. I also knew that a kid down the street named Bobby had a father, and my babysitter across the street had a father. I didn't care too much either way; it was just cool to say that I had one too, I guess.

One day I asked my grandmother about my father. She had a big smile on her face when she told me a story. When I was approximately a year old, my father came to visit me. He put me on his foot and started bouncing me up and down. This sounded cool so far.

"He bounced you for awhile and then you peed on his foot!" My grandmother started laughing. My young mind, however, told me he didn't come back to see me because I pissed on him. Looking back on it now, I think that was the first time I felt shame and guilt as a kid. I carried that for a long time.

There was a unsteady vibe in the house until we moved to Shaker Heights, at the end of my second grade year. I left Rosedale Elementary in Cleveland without much fanfare. I had one very good friend, Bobby, that I haven't seen or heard from since we moved away. There would be no more mention of my father by anyone until I started high school.

MY MOTHER, Inez C. Hall, was born in 1927 to Inez Anderson Hall and Dr. William Myron Hall. She has one brother, William, who currently lives in Virginia with his wife, Audrie.

Inez received her undergraduate degree from Howard University, and a masters in Education from Case Western Reserve University. She loved to play piano, travel, and do Tai Chi. While the family lived in Chicago, she married a man named Percy, who died from a heart attack early in their marriage. After the Hall family moved to Cleveland, she met Clayton Smeltz, my father, at Karamu House where they were both performers. I would later learn that my parents were married before I was born but divorced when I was an infant. From what I'd heard about him, Clayton was given up for adoption, as he was the offspring from an affair his mother had. At my mother's suggestion, he began to use the stage name Clayton Corbin. He settled in New York, and performed with Merv Griffin, James Earl Jones, Maureen Stapleton, Robert Loggia, Lauren Bacall, and many others.

Clayton was mentioned in various articles and books.

From *The Life of Langston Hughes; 1941-1967, I Dream a World* by Arnold Rampersad:

> On May 27 that year, 1954, when he watched a group of young actors, former members of the Karamu Theatre in Cleveland, perform a two-hour program at the Countee Cullen library on the history of Negro playwrights, he felt poignantly the difference between his age and their own. The stars of the show were "an amazing new talent," twenty-four-year-old Clayton Smeltz (later Clayton Corbin), and the self-possessed narrator ("cullud in spite of his name"), Raoul Abdul, only a year older. To Langston, sitting bashfully in the shadows at the back of the room, the evening brought bittersweet memories of "the old library in the days of the '20s," during his first years in Harlem. He saw his youthful self reborn in the performers, and his adult self watching the promise of black youth as some older patron – the bibliophile Arthur Schomburg, or Dr. Du Bois, or even Alain Locke (who died less than two weeks later) – might have done way back then. It seemed to him "really one of the most interesting evenings I've had in Harlem in years." Afterwards, he sent a note of appreciation to Raoul Abdul, who had also written and directed the show, and suggested that it might do well on tour. Late in July, he published a *Defender* column in praise of Clayton Smeltz's talent.

From *Jet* magazine, October 26, 1967:
> Clayton Corbin opened Milwaukee's Repertory season playing
> the moody, harassed and gullible moor, Othello with blond Erika
> Slezak as Desdemona, Marc Alaimo as Iago and Robert Benedetti
> as director.

The next time I heard anything about Clayton was in 1969 or '70. My mother said he was coming to town and would be in the play "Telemachus Clay." I saw him perhaps four times in my life that I recall: three times when he was alive and once when he wasn't. In the '70s when my band I-Tal was starting up and I was in my twenties, Clayton came to Cleveland to be in a production at Karamu, "Dream On Monkey Mountain." *Scene* magazine had written an article about it. While in town, Clayton went with my mother to see I-Tal perform at The Mistake on East 21st and Payne. After seeing the band, and still performing in Monkey Mountain, Clayton went on stage in character and yelled: "I-Tal, I-Tal, I-Tal!"

By 1968, my mother dated Luke Owens, a former defensive tackle with the St. Louis Cardinals. He was tall, dark, and looked threatening. I didn't like him. They eventually married, and I found out later it was mainly because she wanted me to have a father. Owens already had three kids and I wasn't one of them! My mother asked me if I wanted to change my last name to his. I didn't, but said yes, so I became David Owens. He moved us out of my grandparents' house on Onaway into a three bedroom house nearby on Ashwood Road.

Orange Sunshine

During the summer of '69 I started hanging out with white kids I met at Woodbury, and was introduced to hash. These kids drank a lot of beer and smoked Marlboros, but I didn't start smoking cigarettes until I was about 15.

Hashish is the pollen collected from the buds of marijuana and is very potent. When I smoked my first pipeful, I didn't get high. I continued to smoke a few more bowls which caused my eyes to glaze over like I had cataracts! The Woodstock album had just come out so we were listening to Sly and the Family Stone and Hendrix. I couldn't do much more than sit with my mouth open and stare into space. I started buying $20/ounce bags of weed shortly after that, and was introduced to LSD later that summer.

My first trip was on orange sunshine and I loved it. My acid trips usually started out with an anxious feeling leading to my eyes becoming glassy, but this time when I moved my hand in front of my face, I saw a trail from the image of my hand following it like a snake. I'd start to see paisley print all over the place and sure enough, the walls breathed! My sense of hearing seemed to intensify and was accompanied by an occasional echo. The trip, usually lasting about ten hours, was more intense when I smoked weed. I didn't drink much during it 'cause it felt like swallowing something viscious! I would drop acid around 7 or 8 in the evening and stay up until about 6 a.m., when I finally tried to sleep. My eyes always felt dried out from hallucinating. It became a regular thing to do on weekends.

The first time I was introduced to heroin was in high school around 1972. A high school friend and future bandmate went with me and friends Tim and Michael to see Miles Davis at The Smiling Dog Cafe on West 25th. Tim and Michael scored some heroin and snorted the majority of it. Both nodded out at the table, while we drank beer and watched Miles play for 15 to 20 minutes. I later went to the bathroom and saw Miles in a nearby corner with shades on, his head down like he thought he was invisible. I asked him if he was going back onstage, and he mumbled in a voice that sounded like gravel on sandpaper: "I ain't got paid yet!" He didn't go back onstage, but his band was hot.

I WAS SUPPOSED to graduate from high school in 1973, but didn't have enough credits. My counselor, Mr. Looney, advised me to take a typing class during the summer so I'd have enough credits to graduate. I found out later that the class was not credited, and I would have to make up the credit the following year. During this time, my grandfather, Dr. William Hall, a general practitioner, died as a result of cancer, and trauma resulting from a beating he suffered at his practice on East 105th by guys looking for money and drugs. My mother and grandmother asked me to help clean out his office, where I swiped a bunch of Seconals (barbiturates), and a 1,000-count bottle of strawberry-flavored amphetamine sulfate, which I sold out the trunk of my grandfather's 1970 Ford Fairlane. I gave some away and ate most of what was left. I ate so much speed that I had dried white saliva around the corners of my mouth and sores inside from biting my cheeks. (My mouth was always moving and I would bite to stop talking.) That ended when my mother opened the trunk of the car one day and found about a hundred little pink pills lying near the spare tire.

I moved into my grandmother's house in nearby Beachwood because I was uncomfortable living with my mother and stepfather in Shaker. I had more freedom as I lived in the basement, where I drank beer, smoked pot, and tripped on acid. I listened to Hendrix, Pink Floyd, Johnny Winter, Larry Coryell and others through headphones cranked up high. I had a massive record collection that boasted some out-of-print LPs, and later, many hard to find reggae albums. I was proud of my collection of at least 300 albums, all of which I sold some twenty years later to Record Revolution to get money to buy crack. I spent a tremendous amount of time in the basement, teaching myself to play guitar. The night my grandfather died, I dropped acid with two friends, and went to the Miles Drive-In to see the movie *Ben.*

During high school, my mother divorced my stepfather, and my name reverted back to Smeltz. My stepfather told the Shaker school administration that I lived in Beachwood, and they in turn told my mother that I couldn't graduate unless I lived in Shaker. My mother found an apartment for me for the remainder of the school year near Shaker Square. The party was really on now! I don't know how I graduated, but I did in 1974. That September, I went to Ohio State University, and majored in tapping kegs of beer. I lived on the 21st floor of Morrell Tower in a quadrant of four rooms with 2-3 people in each room, and a shower room. I found people who liked to party like me, and quickly found those who sold weed and speed.

One of my roommates was from Valdosta, Georgia. He played a Yamaha acoustic guitar and I accompanied him on harmonica. He taught me the names of the chords I had learned in my basement, and even a couple of new ones. We drank and played and sometimes went to class. I went to see local bands, like a great guitarist named Dave Workman, and I got the music bug! I became friends with members of The Red Mountain String Band, and they allowed me to hang around and play harp with them on occasion. They had a female singer that could wail on some Patsy Cline! I left OSU after two quarters with a GPA of about .75. I never went back.

By early 1976, I was back in Cleveland working at Qua Buick and playing house with my girlfriend. I subsequently worked as a carwasher and later a salesman at Shaker Saab, where I met some sales people who liked to eat speed and drink. I could drink massive amounts of alcohol when I was speeding. We drank at Settler's Tavern on Buckeye Road down the street from a Hungarian mom and pop store where I used to buy beer while underage. Eventually, I was fired from Saab for wrecking a new car. My girlfriend had an abortion, and I didn't support her financially or emotionally. We separated shortly after, and I started working for Snappy car delivery.

CHAPTER TWO

The Roots of I-Tal

MY FRIENDS Bob Caruso, Ralph Tubbs, Arthur Dietz and I had a practice space above the Coco Lounge on 71st and Euclid. Sometime in the late 1970s we played "open mike" night at the Coach House in Cleveland. The owner, Dave Valentine, liked reggae. Dave and I talked later that evening over a lot of free beer, and he introduced me to Gair Linhart, who lived above the Coach House. Dave replaced Arthur on bass, and Gair played Farfisa organ and harmonica. Bob Allen from another reggae band, Terra Plane, came to play drums for us, and John Wagner joined on lead guitar. Dave introduced me to Jamaican-born George Gordon, who played percussion soon after. We had unlimited access to free beer at the bar, and became the house band. There was a banner that hung over the front door of the Coach House that read HOME OF I-TAL.

I never drank when we played because I wasn't able to flow and direct the band. It also slowed me down. Drinking was saved for the end of the night to wind down and mellow out. I smoked a lot of herb while playing and later snorted coke before performing, but didn't drink. Some time later I had a beer while playing and did a 15-minute guitar solo (not a very good one either), which reminded me why I shouldn't drink onstage. I didn't know it then but I was trying to control something that was already out of control. I always knew that after we stopped playing, I could drink as much as I wanted... like a reward for playing my ass off.

Most of us went to Jamaica for a week in January 1978: Dave Valentine, Gair Linhart, John Wagner, Bob Caruso, Bob's brother Ray, a friend named Tony and myself. We drove from Cleveland to Miami, and flew Air Jamaica from there to Montego Bay. I tried magic mushroom tea for the first time from Mrs. Brown's on Negril Beach. It was like tripping on some good acid, with toned down hallucinations. I was also introduced to ganja bread which I ate for breakfast, lunch and dinner. It was like coconut cake (coco bread), with weed baked into it. Very tasty and potent. There was also plenty of white rum and Red Stripe beer available before we returned to the States.

WE PLAYED a New Year's Eve show at the Coach House December 31, 1979 that was recorded live on air by Peter Petto for WRUW. I was introduced to cocaine at Ohio University in Athens by a guy who owned a club named Swanky's. We started playing at Swanky's in late '79 or early '80, and the first night we played, we were invited to a biker party after the gig. They had lines of coke on a mirror and some guy told me to go ahead and do a line, my first time snorting coke. A couple of us stood by the mirror all night after that! As soon as more coke hit the mirror we snorted it up. After that night, I asked bar owners and staff where I could buy some. I was able to drink all night long after the gig without getting tired or woozy. It was the perfect companion for alcohol. Athens was also known as an area for growing some of the best sinsemilla in the US. All of the growers would come to see us play at Swanky's and toss big buds of their best plants to us onstage and off. We never paid for weed...it was *always* free.

Chris Dunmore and Carlos Jones joined around this time, and we gradually began to tour more. We met Phil Alloy in Athens who owned a company, Sinbad, which distributed our first album, and specialized in reggae gear. He was also connected in some way with Bob Marley's wife, Rita. Phil's brother in-law wanted to book some gigs for us and we started touring north and southeastern states. We were the first reggae band from Cleveland to tour extensively. So much, in fact, that Dave Valentine wanted to play more locally, probably because he didn't want to be away from his new wife. Steve Mauer joined to play horn for a short time, and Dave was replaced along with John Wagner and Bob Allen.

Mike "Chopper" Wasson came onboard as lead guitarist, and he and his friend, Gino Long, switched between bass and guitar for a short time. Due to creative differences in 1984, Mike, Carlos, Steve, Bob Caruso, and

Ron Jarvis went on to form the band, First Light, while I-Tal added members from Satta, Buddy Hammond and Billy Coakley[1]; and Dave Lyons, Al Morgan, and Bill Haley from Columbus. The band[2] continued to tour extensively, staying on the road for a month or two at a time. I found a connection for coke in almost every city, as it wasn't difficult to find in the food and beverage industry. Bartenders and servers kept the same hours as musicians, so they partied with us.

MY CIRCADIAN CYCLE had changed. Most days proceeded as follows: Drive – sometimes 10 hours – to the first gig of the tour; arrive at 7 pm; set up by 8; do a sound check; go to the motel to shower and change; go back to the venue at 10 p.m.; and perform three one-hour sets with two half hour breaks. The last set usually lasted longer than an hour though, until 2 a.m. or later. The bar kicked the people out (except the cute girls and dealers), and and some of us would drink until early in the morning. Other members went back to the rooms. I would go to some after hours clubs or homes of bartenders and club people to party: drinking, smoking herb, and snorting coke. If I got back to the motel room it was when the sun was coming up or later. I'd pass out around 11 a.m.; awake by five; vomit; try to eat something by 7 p.m.; find some coke before the show to get rid of the hangover; play at 10 p.m.; and start all over again. Sometimes we'd play one nighters between week-long gigs. The process was largely the same except we'd have to check out of the motel by 11 a.m., which always sucked. I tried to save some blow for those mornings because I knew the hangover would be bad along with my attitude.

I threw up whenever I became conscious. At first it scared me, but soon became the normal thing to do when I opened my eyes. This scenario varied little from 1981 to '92. I played with different band members during this span of time, but the lifestyle seldom varied. Except, perhaps, to do more coke and add heroin.

---

[1]Ellie Nore, vocalist and keyboardist (1979-1985), was instrumental in our promotion and tours. [2]Phil Myriks, Keith McFerin, Doc Smith, Camye Brown, Davey Fields (most from Kent, Ohio) along with sax players Tony Moore and Wayne Preston were members of the last touring formation of I-Tal.

CHAPTER THREE

Spiraling out of Control

AROUND 1987, heroin and I crossed paths again, this time through a female bartender at a club in Dayton, Ohio. I asked her if she could get some for me and we met a friend of hers at a poolroom the next day. I spent about 80 bucks, and the dealer said that he liked customers like me that spend money. I thought it was a compliment!

I snorted that day and into the evening. That night we drove 10 hours from Dayton to Hilton Head Island, South Carolina for a show the next evening. I drank a twelve pack and snorted the rest of the smack. We arrived in Hilton Head around 4 p.m. the following day and rented hotel rooms. I was too high and spaced out to perform. That was the first time the band had to play without me, and the first time I got dope sick. I didn't know it at the time but I was detoxing from the heroin. I thought I had the flu. By this time, the only original members of I-Tal still in the group were George Gordon and me.

From then on, I would try to cop heroin while on the road. I ran into it a few more times, especially in Dayton, but not consistently. We played out of town for months at a time, and basically, lived on the road. We had a booking agent named Greg Demetriatus, who was a friend of our sax player, Tony Moore. Greg contacted beach clubs in Negril, Jamaica, including Arthur's Golden Sunset. When we got to Arthur's, the owner said there shouldn't be a problem booking us at other places. He was right, but he forgot to mention we'd be playing for food and beer! (Which was fine with me, actually!) We played four or five places while there, and shared the stage with Sugar Minott, Joseph Hill, The Mighty Diamonds, and others. After playing a couple of gigs we started to acquire some hangers-on who would say they were with the band, supply us with herb, and find themselves on stage with us.

There was a kid named Little Briggy who would sing some songs with us, and a guy named Fire, who once ripped off a tourist for a half ounce of crack cocaine. Fire promptly delivered the stolen rock to me and two other members so we could help him smoke the evidence. I spent most of the remaining time in Jamaica sitting and sweating in a shack with a tin roof smoking close to pure coke, in 100+ degree temperatures. I would take short breaks to stick my head out of the shack into 80 degree weather to cool off for a second before going back in for more. I left Jamaica with absolutely no money. I had to sell some of my pedals and gear to pay for the taxi to the airport in Montego Bay. I heard that our friend, Fire, is deceased now.

THE NEVER-ENDING FLOW of alcohol and coke continued. While driving through Pigeon Forge, Tennessee, we stumbled upon a Go Kart track. The whole band got out and we decided to ride. We found out that the two guys running the track were selling peach moonshine in little quart-sized jars with screw-on tops. While I held a Dixie cup of the stuff, my feet and sandals got wet as the moonshine was eating through the cup!

I bought two jars immediately.

The owners asked us to leave eventually because we couldn't keep the karts on the track; it was more fun slamming into each other. We played in Augusta, Georgia for the next two nights, during Masters Golf weekend. I went to party with friends of the owner after the first night. They gave me a little less than a half ounce of coke and told me to share it with the band. *Yeah, sure.*

I snorted most of the coke and drank the rest of the moonshine into the next day. Before I knew it, it was time to play at the club again. I was poured into a car and guided toward the stage. I couldn't pick up my guitar, and someone in the audience shouted: "He's drunk!"

I plowed through the show, very ashamed. *I can't wait for this to be over so I can get a drink.* After we played the last song, the bar owner brought over a mini bottle of Cuervo and a Heineken, and said: "Good job."

Not long after, I found myself depressed over a girl I was in lust with. I-Tal left Augusta, Georgia and went on to do a show in Hilton Head. The girl I wanted to see was still in Augusta, so I took a bus back there. After consuming enormous quantities of alcohol and coke, I called a girlfriend in Cleveland and asked her to fly me home. She sent a ticket.

I ate three tabs of ecstasy that my friend Buddy had on the bedside table in the motel room, and flew back to Cleveland. The rest of the band, still in Hilton Head, didn't know I was gone. I simply didn't show up for gigs. The last thing they knew was that I had taken a bus to Augusta.

My girlfriend in Cleveland picked me up from the airport and took me to a motel on Brookpark Road, where she was a dancer. (Did I say she was married?) After she made sure I was in the room safely, she brought me a big tumbler of Cuervo. When the band returned to Cleveland, we started playing again as if nothing had happened.

Circa 1990

I met my future wife in Charleston, South Carolina. I-Tal was playing Halloween weekend and there was a costume contest between sets. She was really cute, dressed as a cowgirl with short shorts, and I fell in lust again. We started talking and hanging out. She was 15 years younger than I, going to school at the local college, and had an apartment. She invited me to her place to watch TV. One thing led to another, and I was soon getting her into the club to see us with her fake ID. I took her hostage onto the road with us for the southern tour.

Back in Ohio, I had been drinking and partying day and night. I lived in Kent for a bit at a band house that we had with our road manager, Tony. At this point, I had left I-Tal, but they continued to play using the name without me. I called a few of the clubs, threatening to sue them if they continued to book them as "I-Tal." (As if I had a lawyer!) George Gordon stayed with the band. I knew he had to earn a living, but it still pissed me off. The band changed the name to Harambe and continued to play gigs where we had played as I-Tal, stating that they were the majority of former members of I-Tal, just as First Light had done years before.

I had a lot of time on my hands, and a house in which to party. I spent most of my days drinking alone, playing guitar in my room, and hooking up with girls at the local bars who could drink like me.

I moved into my mother's condo in Aurora, Ohio not long after, and stayed in her guest room. One night I threw an empty Tequila bottle under the bed and heard a bunch of bottles rattle. I looked under the bed to find many empty beer bottles and a few empty fifths of Cuervo and Mescal. *Where did these bottles come from?* After some serious thought I realized that I was the only one staying in that bedroom, and my mother didn't drink. By process of elimination I reasoned that they must have been mine, although, I had a difficult time believing it. *Must have been there for a long time, and I just added to them.* No one could drink that much in such a short time!

I RAN MY GRANDMOTHER'S '73 Pontiac into a ditch in Aurora, where it got stuck. While gunning the engine in an attempt to get out, the grass underneath the car caught fire. I extinguished the flame with a can of beer I was drinking, and walked back to the condo. Then the police called: the car was on fire.

Another time while my mother was out of town, I was drinking a bottle of Cuervo and watching TV when I ran out of cigarettes. The closest store was ten minutes away on Route 43. A commercial came on and I bet myself that I could get smokes and be back before the last commercial ended. Driving a Nissan my mom helped me buy two weeks earlier, I flew out of the driveway onto Frost Road to the store. I got my Marlboros, and drove back down the hill to the condo. I was doing well until I misjudged the distance to Frost Road where the road T-boned. I drove straight between two light poles, through a wooden fence, and into a pond. I got out of the car, which was floating, and waded to shore.

I was drunk, it was dark out, and I wandered around for more than an hour trying to find my way home. Every time I saw headlights coming, I'd jump off the road into bushes to hide in case it was the police. I spotted a cop sitting on Waldon doing paperwork in his car. I recognized him as the landlord of the house where I had lived in Kent. To frame the picture for you: I'm soaking wet with long dreadlocks covered in leaves and twigs, limping up to the cop's car, and knocking on his window in the dead of night. I scared the bejesus out of him.

"Don't shoot! I used to rent from you!" I shouted. After he stopped yelling at me, he pointed me in the direction of my mother's condo. As I hopped away he yelled after me.

"I should have shot your ass!"

I twisted my ankle to the point that I thought it was broken, but continued to hobble down the road and into the bush as necessary. To add insult to injury, I must have jumped into poison ivy because I had red bumps all over my body, and was scratching like crazy. The police called.

"Do you own a red Nissan?" someone asked. I said I did. "Most of it is submerged in a lake."

They were pissed because they thought I was still in the vehicle when they found it. To me, they sounded a little upset that I wasn't!

Welcome Addition

Now living in an apartment on Mayfield Road near Coventry, I drank nightly at a bar across the street named Bob's, after I was off probation for a DUI. My girlfriend worked to pay for my drinking. She grew tired of the routine and went back to her hometown in South Carolina. Three weeks later, she called and said she was pregnant.

I was living in the same neighborhood, in a third floor attic when I received the call. I encouraged her to come back to Cleveland. After considering it for a bit, she arrived by bus from South Carolina, and I told my new girlfriend that she had to go.

I DECIDED to stop drinking, and actually did for a little more than four years. I wanted to be a good father to my child, and I knew I couldn't be if I continued to drink. We set up a crib in the bedroom and applied for welfare and WIC. Welfare provided food stamps and a small monthly check, and WIC supplied formula and baby food.

I played some gigs as I-Tal around town with John Wagner and Dave Valentine, mainly at The Rhythm Room (formerly Peabody's Cafe) in Cleveland Heights, The Gazette in Seven Hills, and Ozzie's in Kent. At the end of the second set at The Rhythm Room, the manager said I had a phone call. It was my expectant girlfriend: her water had broken. I asked her if she could wait until we finished the third set, to which she reluctantly said yes.

After the show, I took her to Mount Sinai Hospital, and stayed with her that night. In late March, 1992, we welcomed our daughter. I cut the umbilical cord and they handed the baby to her mother. It was the most wonderful day of my life; I will never forget it. I was on the phone with my girlfriend's father in South Carolina, giving him the play by play, until I dropped the phone when the baby emerged! The afterbirth was another story....

After things settled down and she got a private hospital room, I saw two pills on her bedside table, Tylenol #3 with codeine for pain. I asked her if she was going to take them, but she said they made her dizzy. I swallowed them with her water that was bedside, to her amazement. I was no longer drinking, but still consumed mood altering drugs. I reasoned that alcohol was the problem; not weed, pills or a line or two of coke once in a while.

We took our new baby to my mother's condo in Aurora and chilled there in the guest room for awhile. My mother had made a big banner that she hung in the living room, welcoming her first grandchild. We stayed there for a couple of weeks to get used to caring for our baby, then went back to my third floor apartment on Eddington, which consisted of two bedrooms, a bathroom and a combination living room/kitchen. We lived on public assistance and I gigged with a scaled down version of I-Tal: Dave Valentine, John Wagner, Bob Caruso, Chris Desantis, August Oswald, Russ Richards and Irene Mraz.

In September 1992, my girlfriend and I enrolled at Cuyahoga Community College metropolitan campus. We took prerequisites for two years, then applied for the two year degree programs. Using vouchers, we sent our daughter to the on-campus daycare. My girlfriend enrolled in the occupational therapy assisting program, while I took physical therapist assisting.

My mother moved to Cleveland Heights onto East Overlook, with the intention of selling the house to us after we'd graduated. I asked my girlfriend to marry me by placing an engagement ring in a gift box Christmas 1994. The ring cost about $100, as that was all I could afford. We married four days later on December 29, a cold and windy day, at the courthouse. Her father, my mother, and our daughter attended. We had lunch at Hornblowers afterward – we were the only people there!

Graduation arrived in 1996 (me, summa cum laude), and we walked across the stage together at The Wolstein Center. Although they were divorced, my wife's mother and father both came to the graduation from South Carolina, each bringing a new husband and girlfriend respectively. Her sister and grandmother also attended. We were both employed before graduation in the facilities where we did our clinical work for school.

The day after graduation we had a party at our new home. I asked some members of the band to play for the party: Bob Caruso, Dave Valentine, Sean Carey, and John Wagner. We played in the garage while friends and neighbors danced in the driveway. I bought a lot of beer and wine for the party.

I did not drink alcohol for approximately four years, as I had stopped shortly after the baby was born. *I just won't drink that much,* I reasoned as I opened an Amstel Light and drank it. Then I opened another. When the Amstels were gone, I drank Budweiser. I finished the Buds and went for a bottle of Champagne.

"It's not that I mind you drinking, it's just when you do, you drink too much," my wife said at the end of the night.

Somewhere between the Budweiser and Champagne, I told my wife I had to buy cigarettes. I took off to buy some crack at the top of Superior Hill, and smoked it on the way back. I was up drinking Champagne into the early morning. My wife's family was leaving early the same morning and I was unable to get out of bed. I had an extremely bad hangover, and threw up a few times. I made up for four years being dry in one evening.

CHAPTER FOUR

Off and Running

SHORTLY AFTER GRADUATION, since we were working, we went down to the welfare office to tell our caseworker that we wanted to be taken off of welfare and food stamps.

"What do you mean taken off?" she asked. We explained that we had graduated from school, started working, and didn't require assistance anymore. She began to call other people over to her desk. "They want to be taken off because they're working!" A couple of people clapped. "You have to understand, we don't see too many people ask to be taken *off of* welfare!" she said. "Congratulations!"

We saved up enough money to buy the house from my mother. Our daughter started kindergarten at Coventry Elementary in Cleveland Heights, and my mother moved into a condo in Richmond Heights. I attempted to limit my alcohol and crack consumption to weekends. Gradually, I started drinking on Thursday nights and then on an occasional Wednesday.

My second daughter was born in April, 1997. By this time I was working at MetroHealth Skilled Nursing East, next to Tri-C's eastern campus. While at Metro, I had a connect with an employee who would give me her 10 milligram Valiums, Tylenol #3s, and Percocets on occasion. They took the edge off while I worked and would abate any hangover that I may have had.

The patient load at Metro was diverse and I learned to work with a full range of diagnoses: from bedside to obese; brain injury to amputee. I had a female patient that I was teaching to walk again. She had ulcers on her legs but she never seemed to be in too much pain. As a matter of fact, she gave me her pain meds, Dilaudid and morphine tabs on occasion. We became good friends! For all the pain meds she was giving me, I wondered how she kept her own pain in check. One day she introduced me to her husband who asked me if I did "dog food." I knew he was talking about heroin. Now it made sense why my patient didn't miss her meds – she had her own Dr. Feelgood! And yes, we too became good friends.

I started buying occasional sacks of dog food from this guy and took it home to snort it. Sometimes I would meet him down on 79th and Cedar to cop from him. Eventually his wife was discharged from Metro. I started using more often, and I knew he was taking some dope out of the sack before he gave it to me, but I didn't have any other connection. The more I used, the more dope sick I got when I tried to quit. I'd try to stop by drinking more beer and smoking more crack. It got to the point that as soon as I got home after I copped, I'd go straight to the bathroom and use. There was a time when my girls would be in the driveway waiting for me to come home from work. I'd alternate putting one of them on my lap and let her pretend to drive up the driveway and into the garage. They got a big kick out of it and I did too. That all stopped when I started using more. I'd bypass them in the driveway and head for the bathroom. One day, my connect took me to the place where he got his dope: East 105th and Adams. At one point, there would be five or six guys on one block reaching into crevices and bricks on the sides of stores pulling out heroin to sell. It was like an open air market. I never made contact with my old connection after this discovery; I had eliminated the middle man!

WORKING AT METRO became a job within a job. Shortly after I started snorting I had no problem doing without for a day. I'd feel a little nauseous and anxious, but not too bad. I found myself snorting mostly on weekends at first and then weekdays after work. Then I added weekdays at lunch. Finally, I had to cop before I went to work. I started waking up with horrible dry heaves every morning and feeling like I had the flu. My muscles would ache until I was able to snort dope. Eventually, my entire lunch hour was devoted to driving to East 105th to cop and then driving back to work. I would eat Snickers bars from the vending machine for energy throughout the day. When the heroin wore off, I'd start to get sleepy and weak, so the candy bars helped me to be more alert. I also had a prescription for Darvocet that I kept refilling. I'd eat a handful of those when I started to feel sick during the day at work or when I couldn't get away to score more dope. They held the sickness off but only for about ten minutes at a time.

On Halloween, 1997, my wife received a phone call from the New York Police Department: Clayton Corbin had died. They had gotten our phone number from a card that was open on a desk in his apartment. I didn't know that my wife had sent a card to my father with a picture of the girls. They asked if I was next of kin. I thought about it.

"I think I'm the only kin."

I was asked to claim the body.

My mother gave me money to go to Manhattan and to have my father cremated. Before we left town, I stocked up on a bundle (about twelve bags) of heroin for the trip. I also made a stop by our family physician and told her the news. I stated that I was distraught and anxious, knowing that she would prescribe something. She did.

I placed Xanax .25 milligrams under my tongue to dissolve which allowed me to feel the effect more rapidly. For the week and a half I was in New York handling the arrangements for my father, I was loaded. This was the fourth time in my life that I had seen him. I was good and numb – exactly the way I wanted to be.

Upon my return to work, I was assisting in the transfer of an obese patient. She slipped on her way from the treatment mat back to the wheelchair, and I twisted my back trying to prevent her from hitting the floor. It was painful, but more than that, I saw the perfect opportunity to get time off from work and score big on pain meds! Since I was injured on the job, I was able to get workers compensation. I was set up with physical therapy at Metro main campus on West 25th and given an appointment for pain management. The doctor read my chart and asked me what my symptoms were. With my knowledge of back disorders from having written a paper on low back pain and disc protrusion, I presented a possible disc herniation. He suggested three things that he could prescribe for pain:

1) Percocet
2) Oxycodone (Vicodin)
3) Methadone

I quickly chose door #3! He told me that they were just starting to use methadone for severe pain management, and I assured him that I had severe pain. I knew that methadone was also used to keep addicts from getting dope sick. Now I could detox from heroin by myself and no one would ever know that I had been using it. It sounded great in theory but worked lousy in reality! I had a script for 90 tabs per month (cost only $1.20 with Metro health insurance!). It wasn't long before I would melt them under my tongue and snort heroin simultaneously for a better buzz. So much for self-detoxing.

After being off from work for a few months, I decided not to return to Metro, signing instead with the rehab company where my wife worked. I started traveling to and from different facilities, my heroin and crack use still in effect. I tried hard not to use during working hours, to no avail, and even went to the family doctor again. This time I told her I was depressed. (I was depressed mostly because work was getting in the way of getting high like I wanted/had to.) She prescribed Paxil, which I wanted to use to wean myself off of heroin and crack. I reasoned that if these "happy" pills would make me feel good, perhaps I could just take them exclusively. The Paxil did help with my depression: I was a very happy junkie! I smiled and greeted people at work like I was Ronald McDonald at a new restaurant opening. Another lesson I learned: happiness does not cure addiction! I discovered much later that happiness is a by-product of abstinence, working the 12 steps, and learning to live at peace with myself.

I knew it was wrong for me to use at work, but, by this time, the call of the drug was more powerful. I'd find myself going out to my car numerous times while at work, ducking down behind the steering wheel, putting a piece on the stem and smoking it. Immediately I'd feel a sense of calm, relief, and a second wind which was short lived. It seemed that as soon as I would start to walk back into work I'd have an urge to go back to the car and take "just one more" hit. I progressed to smoking inside the facilities, all the time knowing my job and patients were at risk.

Eventually, I stopped going to work. Partially out of guilt, but mostly from an insatiable urge to use. It was no longer about smoking and snorting to get high; I now had to use in order to *function* throughout the day. I was losing a lot of weight, so I tried to convince my wife and the PTA parents that perhaps I had cancer. A friend of my wife's suggested celiac disease, so I ran with that diagnosis for awhile. I started going in for upper and lower gastrointestinal tests, yet they found nothing. I continued to lose weight. At 134 pounds, my doctor at Metro told me that if I lost two more pounds he would admit me into the hospital. My wife bought a pair of jeans for me earlier in the week because all my clothes were not fitting anymore. The jeans she bought were a little baggy when I put them on. They were size 28.

The next day I complained about feeling sick and very weak. (I was dope sick; I ran out of heroin, methadone and crack.) My wife put me and our daughters into the minivan and drove to Metro main campus. I was in the passenger seat, reclined, when all of a sudden my wife screamed and hit me on my arm.

"Why did you do that?" I asked. She had glanced over at me and saw that I was pale, and my eyes were half open. She thought I was dead.

I was taken to the emergency room, and after they called my doctor, I was admitted. The nurse asked what medications I had been taking.

"Methadone!" She asked if I was a heroin addict. "No, it was prescribed for my back secondary to a bulging disc." She left to check with the attending physician and came back shortly.

"We don't have methadone so the doctor prescribed morphine." A big smile came to my face.

"That should be fine!"

I was there for two or three days, and ate everything in sight. The doctor and nurses couldn't figure out how a guy who appeared to be severely malnourished could be stuffing his face so much. It had been one of the first days that I hadn't smoked any crack. When smoking rock, I didn't eat. Every time I would get a hunger pang I'd smoke more to stave off the hunger. This way I didn't have to take time to eat. Now that I had some down time I could eat as long as the morphine kept me mellow. I was sure that the doctor would find cocaine in my system via the bloodwork that had been performed. I had reconciled myself to the truth being brought to light and then, no matter how embarrassing, I could get some help. The last thing I was going to do was tell anyone that I was a crackhead! I would tell them that I had a cocaine problem when they confronted me.

They never confronted me because they weren't testing for drugs. I realized later that they wouldn't test for opiates because they were giving me liquid morphine. They tested for everything but drugs and only came up with slight anemia. I enjoyed being in the hospital. It was like a vacation. I didn't have to worry about where to get money to cop so I wouldn't get dope sick. I could relax and enjoy that warm hazy morphine buzz while watching TV all day. My wife and children came to visit the first night, and then on the last day to pick me up for discharge home. My wife was upset that they couldn't find anything wrong.

I WAS DISCHARGED home while my Metro doctor scheduled more tests. Meanwhile, my wife was the only one working. During the previous months I had gotten numerous cash advances on our credit card, and was barely paying it back. One day my wife told me that MBNA had called and questioned the ever-growing advances I had been receiving in secret. I had been leaving the house every night like clockwork to cop crack to stave off being dope sick. I could no longer afford heroin, plus I could purchase crack within ten minutes of my home. My prescription for methadone had been decreased and eventually stopped altogether. Although I was forced to detox from heroin I remained dope sick until two months into treatment. It was December, 2000.

Once in treatment I learned that methadone has a long acting life, which means that it stays in your system for a long time after you discontinue its use. That explained why I felt like crap for such a long time. I remember telling one of the monitors at the treatment center: "I thought I was supposed to feel better after I stopped using and now I feel worse!"

One night my oldest daughter asked me to stay home, and I promised her that I wouldn't leave. I really tried to stay, but the call was too strong, and I was getting irritable and restless the more I tried. It got to the point where I knew I would explode if I didn't get something immediately. I told her I'd be right back just as I had many times before. The look in her eyes was heartbreaking, but by now I couldn't stop using. Not for my children, not for my wife, not for my mother and not for me. I had turned into something that I absolutely hated: a liar, thief and manipulator. The guilt I felt being a poor example of a father and husband eased only when I could remain medicated every waking hour. This was a full time job!

I did whatever was necessary in order to maintain. I waited until my wife had gone to sleep, grabbed the keys to the minivan, put it in neutral, let it roll out of the driveway, and started it on the street hoping she wouldn't hear me. I obtained the PIN to her debit card and took out small amounts of cash (mostly 20s) on a regular basis. This culminated into accusing my wife of cheating on me.

CHAPTER FIVE

Domestic Violence

I WAS IN COURT on a charge for a domestic violence after my wife and I had a fight and a broom I kicked hit her ankle. A temporary restraining order was placed on me so that I could not speak to her, nor be within 500 feet. A second order was placed restricting contact with my two daughters. The second order stemmed from a Christmas visit with my oldest daughter. By this time, I was out of our home and living at my mother's. I bought presents with the last $250 available on our Visa, and wanted to give them to my daughters. My mother went to pick up the girls, but my youngest had a cold and couldn't go. When my oldest arrived, I gave her the gifts. I was very high. I told her that her mother was trying to set me up, that she had people trying to kill me, and would take them away from me. I scared her so much that she locked herself in the bathroom and wouldn't come out. I believed that what I was telling her was the truth. My mother was able to coerce her out, and said I should be ashamed for scaring her. My mother drove my daughter back home.

Around the time when the second restraining order was issued barring me from having contact with my daughters, I started having hallucinations. I believed that I saw numbers on pieces of paper and that they were scratched into the woodwork of my mother's home. I collected pieces of paper hoping to convince someone that my wife was trying to run some kind of credit card fraud scheme on me. (Later, I learned this to be cocaine-induced psychosis.) I was able to speak to my daughters only through communication with my mother. I'd sit next to my mother who was on the phone with them, and she'd say: "The girls say they love you." I would tell her to tell them that I loved them too. I felt defeated, worthless and beaten. That is, until I could smoke some crack and just say fuck it. The only way I was able to partially deal with the situation was to smoke more dope, and the more dope I smoked the more the situation worsened.

After running up to my mother's bedroom one night with a hammer, sweating profusely, claiming someone was behind the wall in the basement, my mother told me I had to leave her house. She quickly locked her bedroom door, and I ran back down to the basement where I was staying. I began to tear holes in the ceiling, looking for crack rocks that I had stashed for the future.

In January, 2001, I left my mother's house and stayed at various motels and hotels around town. I wanted to get as high as possible to forget about the pain I was causing everyone. There wasn't enough dope to help me forget what was happening. At the time, I thought I was really the victim in all of it. From my wife's purse I had taken the savings book permitting me access to the proceeds of selling our East Overlook home, approximately $14,000. I knew that by having control over the money I would piss off my wife and that's exactly what I wanted to do. I wanted my wife to hurt like I was hurting. Something else I learned later down the road: "hurting people hurt people."

I rented a room at the Travel Lodge on Lake Avenue in Lakewood, and brought with me a supply of crack and heroin. The manager was nice so I bought a package of cookies for him. Later that evening I started ruminating over my wife and missing her. I wanted to let her know how much I loved her and to ask her if we could work things out. Wrong thing to do! I called very early in the morning, and when she answered, I got scared and didn't speak.

"Dave, is that you?" she asked. I mumbled something a couple of times and she said, "You're not supposed to be talking to me!"

I hung up quickly. My wife dialed *69, calling the motel back. She told the manager that I was harassing her, and she was calling the police. The manager returned my cookies and kicked me out. I called my mother from a payphone. She said the police were looking for me, and I should turn myself in, or go to a hospital to get help with my drug problem. When I arrived at the ER of Huron Road Hospital, I told the staff that I was a heavy crack and heroin user and needed help. I was asked to supply urine, lay on a gurney, and they shot me up with something to relax me. I felt like everything was going to be okay: I was in a hospital, under a doctor's care, and hopefully off to safety somewhere. A few minutes later, a Cleveland Heights policeman entered, asked if I was David Smeltz, and said they had been looking for me. I was promptly handcuffed.

At Cleveland Heights city jail, the contents of my pockets – $15, a lighter, car keys – were placed into a plastic bag. My mug shot was then taken, making all of the officers laugh, and they passed it around to other officers in the building for their amusement. I was ushered into a cell where I started to detox from the remaining heroin in my system. After laying down on a concrete slab they called a bed, I became anxious to leave. I called an attorney friend who I had used a few times for DUI arrests.

I first met Tucker years before at the Coach House, when he came on stage and played flute with the band. He was in law school at the time. I called Tucker because another high school friend and attorney, Harry, had become fed up with me. After smoking a bunch of crack one day, I called Harry early in the morning to complain about my wife, which he didn't appreciate because he had a wife and small children at home. I had also called him from Portage County jail on a DUI conviction, complaining that they wanted to keep me longer than the week I had been sentenced to. When I met with Harry to ask him to represent me, he said no. Then I asked him for $5, to which he said: "You need to get some help!" Harry had gotten me out of a lot of jams because of our previous friendship: we partied together in high school, and played racquetball once during the four years I was dry.

Tucker arrived at the jail and looked at me with what I perceived as disgust. He quoted me a price, and said that my mother was bugging him about getting me to sign some paper. The form in question was from the PT/OT board in Columbus, and arrived every two years. I had to prove that I had taken continuing education classes, state where I was working and let them know if I had committed any crimes! I signed it through the cell bars, gave it back to Tucker to give to my mother to mail. I had completely forgotten that I was a physical therapist assistant. Tucker said I'd be out in a couple of hours.

I waited, waited and waited longer. My back began to ache and my nose started running. I felt weaker and my thoughts became cloudy. I was detoxing. All I could think about was the $15 I had and what I was going to do with it when I was released. Tucker had told me that my mother wanted me to go for a psychiatric evaluation immediately upon release. I think I agreed so I could get out sooner.

Finally the time came for my release. They gave me my $15 and other property but all I saw was the money. They released me into my mother's custody, and she drove me to Huron Road Hospital where I had left my car. Along the way she said she was worried that I didn't know what I was doing, and needed help. All I knew at that moment was that I needed some heroin.

My mother dropped me off on the first floor of the parking garage, and I walked up to the second floor to find my car. It was a very cold day so I prayed for my car to start. It did. I cruised down to the first floor, down the ramp and past my mother who was waiting to follow me to the psych eval. As I passed her, I saw an expression on her face that I've never forgotten: hopelessness, bewilderment and despair. It was as though I had ripped out her heart. For the first time I realized that heroin meant more to me than the love of my mother.

I PROMISED myself that I would use the $14,000 in the bank sparingly — would take out only half of it. But now I was looking for vindication. I used the money as a way to get back at my wife, who I perceived, had screwed me over, and also to stay high for awhile. I vowed to stay away from the Meadowbrook Road home where my wife and daughters were living, and began taking money out of the account to use for hotel rooms, dope, cigarettes, gas. I started out at fairly nice places. The first overlooked I-271, had a full kitchen, and cost about $100 a day. I don't know why I needed a kitchen because I wasn't hungry after smoking crack. I'd smoke and daydream out the window facing 271. My thoughts raced the more I smoked. I thought I saw our minivan on the highway a few times which started me thinking about my family. I missed my kids, my mother and even my wife. I called information to get my aunt and uncle's phone number. I called them early one morning, ranting about how my wife had run out on me, was cheating, and asked if they would help me. My aunt's reply: "You need some professional help!" I felt let down because I wanted them to side with me and they didn't. My uncle wouldn't even speak to me. It was obvious that they had spoken with my mother.

My mother called crisis intervention and they sent someone over to see if I was crazy. I was able to pass the tests he administered because I had seen them performed at the hospital where I had worked. I knew exactly what he wanted to hear. I was crazy for sure even though I passed the tests! Thinking more and more about my wife, I decided to find out what they were up to. I found a private investigator from Akron in the phone book, told him my wife was cheating on me and I needed evidence to bust her. He said he would start on the case for $500, and I should meet him at a gas station in Akron. I checked out of the motel, immediately withdrew a couple thousand dollars, and drove to Akron after I picked up an eight ball[3] of crack and about six bags of dog food (heroin). I checked into a Holiday Inn at $75/night, and paid extra for a game system in my room. I smoked a little, then went to meet the investigator.

The guy knew I was loaded, and asked for more money stating he didn't know the subject was in Cleveland, therefore, it would cost more. I gave him a another $500 and my room number to the Holiday Inn. He said he would stake out my house on Meadowbrook, and let me know about any men my wife was meeting. Just what I wanted to hear! I told him I'd wait at the motel for updates. Two days passed and I didn't hear

---

[3] An eight ball is 1/8 ounce of coke. At the time, a 20 costed $20 and a 10 piece costed $10. A good 20 is about the size of a grape. Approximately five or six 20s equals an eight ball.

from him. On the third day I called him and asked him what was up. He yelled at me: "Don't call me. I told you I'd call you!" He hung up.

I made a couple of runs to Cleveland for more dope to hold me over. A few more days went by and I called again. He said, "The house looks empty," and hung up. I checked out of the motel and returned to the family home in Cleveland Heights. I drove past the house a few times with caution, as there was still a restraining order in effect, and I didn't want to be arrested for stalking my wife. I noticed there were no tire tracks in the snow on the driveway. Each day I passed the house, I didn't see tracks.

I parked on the street behind our house one day, and went through our neighbors' backyard to the back of our house. I saw an empty box on the patio and no footprints. All of the shades were drawn as I slowly crept up to the back window and peered through the venetian blinds. All of the furniture in the living room was gone! A sick feeling formed in the pit of my stomach and I became anxious. I broke the window, and climbed into the house. Everything was gone. I went upstairs. Our king-sized bed was gone. My daughters' beds, gone. Their toys, gone. I went to the basement and found a daybed, a stereo console my grandmother had given me, a freezer from my mom and an old color TV with the antenna broken off that I used to smoke crack. I sat on the daybed and cried.

CHAPTER SIX

Already Dead

I TRIED TO rationalize the situation by telling myself: *Now that they're gone, I can get high like I want to.* And I proceeded to do just that. More dope, more motel rooms, more mental anguish. The most difficult time was when I'd start to come down from the drugs. When I was the least bit sober, reality would hit me in the face and I couldn't deal with it. I'd spent so many years altering my perception of situations. My solution to any problem or life situation was to drink and use drugs. This way, nothing ever seemed that bad – as long as the substance was working. I never suspected that one day the drugs would stop working sufficiently to mask the truth. I could not stay high every hour of the day and night. And believe me, I tried!

I became extremely paranoid. Later, during an outpatient stint at Metro, the counselors labeled it "cocaine-induced psychosis." I rented a motel room on Northfield Road by the old Ellacott VW place. I made runs all night down to East 105th to cop and then back to the motel. I was slowly running out of money. I became so paranoid that I thought people were following me back to my motel room and waiting to rob me. To remedy this, I drove farther out Northfield and rented another motel room near Rockside Road. I started driving back and forth from one motel to the other in an attempt to confuse my imaginary stalkers. It got to the point that anyone who happened to look my way got the evil eye from me because I knew they were out to harm me in some way. I was the guy who'd drive by and stare at you with a look that said *you're not fooling me, I know you're watching me.*

I had stopped taking showers for awhile now. Brushing my teeth was not a priority either. One day I got into this guy's car to buy some rock.

"Damn, do you smell that?"

"What?" I asked.

"Something smells like shit!" he exclaimed.

"I don't smell nothing," I told him. "Give me a twenty."

"Here man...get out my car. You stink!"

His comment didn't faze me; I had a twenty dollar rock in my hand ready to smoke.

With the bank account shrinking, I attempted to use moderation when getting high, to try to make the dope last longer. I could no longer afford heroin, so my main focus was buying crack. My thoughts were that using crack helped soothe the effects of withdrawal. It did take the edge off of being dope sick, but it only worked when the smoke was in my lungs. I could no longer afford to buy eight balls, so I was buying 20s and putting smaller pieces on the stem. 20s became 10 pieces, and 10s soon became crumbs. I begged guys to pinch off a piece for $2. Most of the dope boys on the block would say: "Get out of here until you find some real money, you crackhead!"

I went back regularly to my empty home, crawled through the window I'd broken, and searched for things to sell so I could buy more crack. I even tried to trade one of my daughter's VHS tapes that I found in the mostly empty house for crack. Not many dope boys wanted a *Free Willy* tape and once again they said: "Get outta here, crackhead!"

One of the last places I stayed was a place off of West 25th called the Jay Hotel. I had enough money to rent an extremely small room with no bathroom and no windows for a week, about $120. By the second day, I asked the manager for some money back because I was going to shorten my stay. I needed money to buy crack. I was very sick when I lived there. I didn't eat for days at a time, had very bad diarrhea, and the bathroom was far down the hall. It was all I could do to make it to the bathroom, especially if I wasn't high. I had no energy unless I smoked some rock. When I got to the Jay, the maintenance guy said he liked me because I wasn't like the other people who lived there. Most of them were so nasty, he said, that they didn't bother going down the hall to use the bathroom they would use the trash cans in their rooms. Before I left the Jay Hotel, I too would urinate and defecate in the trash can in my room.

ABOUT A MILE down West 25th from the Jay Hotel was a plasma donation center that paid $35 for blood plasma. I was very dope sick, and broke, so I decided to head over there to pick up some quick cash. It was the first time I had gone to a place like that, as I was never much for needles. I never mainlined my heroin; always snorted or smoked it. I believe I would have started booting it eventually, because it was taking ever increasing amounts to feel the effects. Directly into my bloodstream would have been more efficient.

I was sitting in the plasma center sweating bullets, stomach in knots, and nose running to the floor waiting to be interviewed to get paid. My name was finally called.

"Have you ever been to prison?" the guy asked when I sat down.

"No," I replied, "just jail."

"Have you ever had anal sex or homosexual relations?"

"No! Definitely not!"

"Have you ever done or consumed any street drugs?"

"I smoked some pot a long time ago."

"Have you ever inhaled or smoked cocaine?"

"Yes."

"How long ago?" He asked. I hesitated.

"Hmmm, probably about...well um, about a year ago...yeah, a year ago." *More like a few hours ago.*

"Ok sir, thank you."

I went to the waiting room, and was feeling worse. I stuck it out only because I pictured someone putting 35 bucks in my hand. I would then go out to cop some dope so I could function without feeling weak and sickly. Everyone's name was called except mine. Eventually I went up to the desk and asked when it would be my turn. She said I had been rejected, and they were wondering why I was still sitting there.

I *really* felt sick. I had become so desperate that I drove to the eastside to snatch rocks from dope boys. The possibility of being shot while grabbing rocks from these guys didn't faze me; I knew that I needed to get high no matter what. I drove to East 105th and up Gooding, where dopeboys flocked my car. At least five put their hands in the window, showing me rocks. I hit their hands and the rocks went flying into my car as I floored the gas pedal, and screeched around the corner. There was a thrill in doing it, and also a reward! I continued to do this in different parts of the city.

There was the time when I had been a frequent customer of a teenager. I always paid him, so he trusted me. I pulled up to him and he greeted me warmly, expecting a sale. He put his hand in the car and showed me a $40 rock. I hit his hand, and the rock flew into my car. He grabbed my shirt as I attempted to go from zero to sixty in a 1984 VW Fox 4-speed. He hit my mouth with a juice bottle and started punching the side of my head with his fist as the car started to gain momentum. He was hanging onto me, and yelled: "I'm gonna kill you, motherfucker!" He couldn't keep up with the speed of the car, so he let go rather than be dragged down the street. I stuck my head out my window and yelled back: "You can't kill me, motherfucker! I'M ALREADY DEAD!"

CHAPTER SEVEN

The Crack Taxi

I WAS OFFICIALLY BROKE. From January to March 2001, I'd spent $14,000. Perhaps there was $30 left in the bank account. I checked out of the Jay Hotel and walked a block down West 25th to a pay phone. I called my mother, started crying and told her I needed help to stop using. I said that I couldn't go to treatment unless my wife and kids were there to support me. She quickly let me know that that wasn't happening! Later down the road of recovery I learned that I had to get clean for me and no one else. I would be setting myself up for relapse if I tried to get sober for someone else. Every time I thought about them I'd break down. Without the drugs to mask my feelings, the reality of my situation was unbearable. I was an emotional mess.

I continued to drive around the inner city, snatching rocks, and giving people rides hoping they would pay me in crack. I humorously called myself "The Crack Taxi." All I wanted was a couple of bucks in my tank (I was living in my car), and some dope if they could get some. I drove by a kid, gave him the nod like I was looking for some dope, and planned to snatch whatever he had. He motioned me into the parking lot of an abandoned building. All of a sudden the kid brandished a brick and threatened to throw it through my front window! He said I snatched a rock from him on Gooding, and if I didn't give him all of my money he was going to destroy my front window. I emptied my pocket, $5 and change, and begged him not to throw the brick. When I gave him the money he said: "Now get the fuck outta here crackhead!" I drove away pissed off. My brain was so scrambled that I was driving around the same neighborhood I'd been snatching from.

I was *broke* broke and needed to get high. I saw some guys on a corner and gave one of them the look. He motioned me over to the curb, but something didn't look right. His hand was under his coat and the rest of his boys were smiling and heading toward my car. He asked me to let him in and I hesitated. All of a sudden a brick came flying at my front windshield and nailed the corner hitting metal mostly, leaving a hairline crack and then ...SMASH!... another brick went through my passenger side rear window. I realized that these were the other guys that I had stolen rocks from. I screeched off and drove to the Cleveland Clinic emergency room. I needed help; it was getting dangerous and I was too tired to try to come up again. I told the receptionist that I was withdrawing from drugs and I wanted to kill myself. I wanted the pain to stop. I was put in a room where I waited for the attending physician.

The doc came in and started to examine me, as I told him my history of heroin and crack use. I was laying on the table when he started poking.

"Does this hurt?" Suddenly he gasped. "Oh, my God! You're so thin that I'm touching the examining table while palpitating your stomach!" This guy was freaked out because he pretty much put his hand right through me from the front to the back. I told him that I needed help and if I had to go back out on the street I'd kill myself. Actually I was too chicken to kill myself – I just wanted the pain to stop – emotionally and physically.

"You want a place to sleep for the night," he said skeptically.

"I will die out there if you discharge me," I insisted. He turned on his heels and walked out. A few minutes later an orderly came in with a wheelchair. *YES! I'm going to treatment!*

I was taken upstairs and put into a room with another patient. The nurse took my vitals and asked how much heroin I had been doing. I knew that the more I stated, the more methadone they would give me. I told them I snorted about eight bags a day (which I did when I had the money), but I was actually scavenging for dope, and warding off dope sickness by smoking crack.

"Judging by these wet sheets, it looks like you're in withdrawal," she said.

I didn't notice my sheets were soaked with sweat. She gave me the first methadone cocktail; eventually, I would be weened down to nothing. I thanked her, lay back in the bed with my hands behind my head and turned to my roommate.

"Hey, this treatment stuff ain't bad!" He turned his head to look at me.

"This ain't treatment – this is the psych ward!" Then, a moment of clarity. The psych ward was where they sent people who said they were going to commit suicide.

Methadone for breakfast, lunch, and dinner while watching TV and ransacking the fridge in the middle of the night was how I spent the next few days. One day they told me I had to go to therapy, so I floated down to the multi-purpose room. The occupational therapist asked if I would like to make a wallet or a moccasin. (*One* moccasin!) I opted to make the wallet, though I had nothing to put in it. I proceeded to tell the OT that I was a physical therapist assistant, and I knew all about ADLs and fine motor skills. She gave me a sarcastic grin.

"Sure, Mr. Smeltz. Let's focus on the wallet."

After two or three days, I was stable enough to go to the treatment floor, although, I was still being weened off methadone. I started receiving one dose in the morning and one before lunch. My first day on the treatment floor, I was taken to my room. A girl was already in there.

"Hey! I'm your new roomie!" I said.

"Nurse?!" she said as she went into the hall. The staff acknowledged their mistake, and put me in a room me with a drunk from West Virginia. I liked the coed arrangement better! Later in recovery I bumped into her at Founders Day in Akron, a celebration of the founding of A.A. We were both sober and laughed about coed treatment. We had become friends during treatment, and she asked if I got the pack of Marlboros she left for me before she was discharged from the Clinic.

"Oh, those were from you?" I said. "Thanks."

I have not seen her since.

My West Virginia roommate was kind. The only thing I brought with me to the hospital besides a bag of dirty clothes was my guitar. My roommate asked if I knew any country tunes, and I proceeded to play "Tennessee Stud" by Doc Watson. The rendition was rough and I couldn't remember most of the words but his eyes lit up. Staring at the big hole on the bottom of my guitar, he asked what had happened. I told him the story about the brick flying through my car window hitting my guitar.

"I might be able to fix that," he said and pulled out a roll of duct tape that he used to mend his duffle bag. He began to apply it to the hole in my guitar, carefully placing layers to cover the hole. "Here, try it now." I strummed it and the sound resonated again. I thanked him. It was the nicest thing anyone had done for me in a long time without wanting anything in return. I felt a camaraderie with him. The next day his family came to take him back to West Virginia. He told me, "Listen to these people, and do what they tell you to do, and you'll be okay." He left the room, and I felt abandoned and alone again. I covered my head with my bed sheet and cried.

There was a doctor at the Clinic named Collins, who was there to supervise and educate us about the disease of addiction. We had to attend daily group therapy with him. He was known for writing down descriptors of us in magic marker and pinning them to our shirts or blouses, and we had to walk around all day wearing them. Nurses and other personnel would continually ask us "What's that mean?" And we'd have to describe how the saying related to us. My coed friend had been sober for a short time and then her mother died suddenly. She said that was why she started drinking again after being dry for awhile. She and her mother were close and I believed she stopped drinking, in part, to please her. Dr. Collins placed a sign on her that read, "What would mama say?" He was trying to get her to acknowledge the fact that her mother (even in death) would not approve of her drinking again. The good doctor had written one for me too. In bold black magic marker he wrote three letters: USC.

He asked if I knew what they stood for. With a big smile I said sarcastically: "University of Southern California!" Without a smile he answered: "No, it stands for Up Shit Creek!" He was right on the money.

One day a staff member came to my room and asked if I was an alcoholic or an addict. At this point, I thought drugs were my only problem. I had completely forgotten about the four or five DUIs I had racked up. I said: "I'm an addict, man." It sounded kind of badass and truthful at the same time. He gave me the Basic Text of *Narcotics Anonymous* and said: "Read the chapter entitled, Who's An Addict?" I had enough trouble putting sentences together in my head let alone trying to read anything. That book stayed closed (along with my mind), until three months later.

Around my fifth day there, my legs started swelling. I informed Dr. Collins and he sent me to my room to wait for the nurse to see me. I lay on my bed for a bit which seemed like eons to me. I began running scenarios in my head about how they didn't care enough about me to take care of my legs. I formed massive resentments toward the people who were trying to help me, and planned ways to show them I was a person that demanded immediate attention. As I look back on this I now understand that my low self-esteem, restlessness and irritability were setting me up for failure. I was given methadone only once a day in a cup that was mostly orange juice. I could tell the difference. Methadone has a long acting life, which means the affects of withdrawal stay around long after you've stopped taking it. I still felt dope sick, and my best thinking told me to leave. I had $10 that my mother dropped off for me to buy snacks. We were allowed to go to the parking garage for 10-minute smoke breaks, so I told the nurse that was where I was headed.

I went to the garage, got in my car, and took off to buy some crack. They weren't medicating me so I took it upon myself to do it. I copped a rock and smoked it. After it was gone, I realized that nothing had changed, and I didn't have anywhere to go. I knew that I had awakened the beast again, and if I didn't go back to the clinic, I'd be back to snatching rocks. I drove back to the clinic and was stopped on my way back to my room.

"Where have you been? We've been looking for you for an hour," the head nurse said. I told her that I might have had some important mail to pick up at my old house, so I went to see. "Did you use while you were gone?" Knowing that they would do a urinalysis, I saved them the trouble and said yes, hoping they'd understand. The nurse said: "Go pack your bag, now. You have to leave!"

Before discharge, I was given a list of places to eat for free, recovery resource services, including churches, and facilities that fed the homeless and provided shelter. My discharge paper read:

Admission Date: 2/3/01
Discharge Date: 2/8/01

Principal Diagnosis: Polysubstance abuse/ dep. (heroin, cocaine)

Other Diagnoses: ASRD, chronic back pain

Follow up
CCF: Follow up AA/NA + get a sponsor
        Aftercare at CCF, Recovery Resources –
        patient to make appointment

I left the Clinic and went directly to my mother's home. I knew that if I made any stops along the way that I'd most likely be stuck for awhile. I told her that the Clinic found out that I didn't have medical insurance so they kicked me out. She couldn't believe their insensitivity toward someone who was (supposedly) trying to get his life in order, and I agreed with her. She said I could stay in her basement as long as I was actively looking for a treatment facility.

"I'll get on it right away!" I said as I went down the basement steps.

She yelled after me: "And don't tear down the acoustic tiling in the ceiling again. I just had it replaced!"

I sat down, took a deep breath, turned on the TV, and began thinking about where I might have stashed something. I looked everywhere. I had an old blown out spare tire from my Volkswagen down there. At one time I stashed some bags of heroin in it when I had money while riding around town getting high. I picked up the tire and put my hand in the long rip on the side by the rim. I felt something. I started shaking the tire, holding it upside down. A small blue sack of heroin fell out. I thought for a second about how I just detoxed from heroin in the past five days, and to start *doing it again would be stupid.* With the last six words still ringing in my head, I tore open the sack as if on automatic pilot, poured the contents on an album jacket, and snorted it. The rush was familiar and missed. Any thought of treatment was gone in an instant. I was off and running again.

I NODDED for a bit in my mom's basement. I told myself that this was the last time, and I would stay there until I was able to get into treatment. The heroin was wearing off and my stomach was beginning to turn with that familiar nauseous, dope sick feeling. It was very early in the morning and I was broke. I promised myself that I wouldn't leave. I was tired of trying to come up all the time. It had become a full time job. I also had a feeling that something horrible was going to happen if I went back out to try to snatch some rocks. A great feeling of dread hung over me. I searched my mother's house for anything to take the edge off of the dope sickness. I found a bottle of Jamaican Rum that I had given to my mom from a visit to the island. It was mostly full. I got a glass, some ice, a can of Coca Cola. I started drinking and smoking Marlboros. I ran out of Coke, but continued to drink. I ran out of ice, yet continued drinking. I passed out. I realized that the best way to stay home was to pass out so that I couldn't leave.

I woke up later that day feeling awful: a hangover and dope sick. My mother pretty much left me alone. Every once in awhile she'd call down to tell me that dinner was ready. It was all I could do to eat anything. I wanted her to think that I was eating, so I would take a plate of food to the basement, and throw it into a bag. I then moved the bag into the garage to be thrown away later. I threw away a lot of food. By early evening, the sickness became unbearable. I began to search again for something to knock me out. I found a bottle of Creme de Menthe, a green colored, peppermint-tasting liqueur. I drank the whole bottle, and puked green vomit that smelled like peppermint! It gave me a buzz, but wasn't enough to put me under. I found an old bottle of coffee liqueur and drank that. I searched a cabinet in the kitchen and found Tylenol PM. I took four of those, and that did the trick until the next day. I knew I couldn't keep that up. I scraped together $6 in change and left the house.

I drove to East Cleveland and found a dope boy that broke off a crumb for six bucks. After I smoked it, I drove to the ER at MetroHealth on West 25th. They gave me Neurontin and clonidine to help with my withdrawal symptoms. I didn't want to go back to my mother's house, so a social worker wrote a letter for me to get into the homeless center at 2100 Lakeside. It stated that I was homeless and was interested in the recovery services that they provided. I arrived at 2100 around 9 p.m. with my guitar. The letter I got from the social worker wouldn't do any good until the next day when staff was there. It was winter and cold outside. My right rear passenger window was still broken, and it was too cold to sleep in my car. 2100 was packed; there weren't any cots or blankets left. I found a spot under a long card table in the back of the hall and lay down with my guitar next to me. I listened to people snore, and smelled the farts and feet of some 70-80 men.

The next day I went back to Metro and signed up for their outpatient program. I got a confirmation slip from them, took it to my mom, and I was back in the basement again waiting to go to outpatient treatment at Metro the next morning at 9 a.m. I knew if I went out this evening I would not make it to outpatient at Metro the next morning. I also knew that if I was able to pass out I could make it through the night. I begged my mother for some money to buy a twelve pack.

"Are you sure you should be drinking?" she asked.

"I don't see why not because I'm staying at home tonight!" I still did not think I had a problem with alcohol, and resented her questioning my rationale. She gave me some money anyway. I bought a twelve pack, took it to the basement and killed it. I passed out early morning and awoke in enough time to make it to Metro by 9:30 a.m. I was a half hour late.

"We thought you weren't gonna show," the receptionist said. I was beginning to hear this phrase more frequently. They made me sit down, listen to the do's and don'ts, gave me a rules and regs booklet, and asked me to sign it, signaling that I understood and agreed. The things that stayed in my head: *coming to class high or intoxicated is grounds for dismissal* and they will *conduct random urinalyses*. The outpatient treatment would last for five weeks with classes to be held Mondays, Wednesdays, and Fridays from 9-3 with an hour for lunch.

I was examined by a doctor and bloodwork was done. Neurontin was again prescribed to soothe my jumpy nerves. When the bloodwork came back, it showed that I was slightly anemic, and had increased liver enzymes working overtime to metabolize the poison I routinely put into my system.

I was taken to a large conference room where I was introduced to approximately eight other clients, both male and female. There was long black chalkboard that covered most of one wall. A staff member was explaining, with diagrams and handouts, the disease of addiction. The patients had varying amounts of clean time: some were ready to graduate while others had been there only a few weeks. I was scared, insecure, and felt extremely out of place. I always needed something to help me feel comfortable in settings like this. Without something to take the edge off I felt totally ill at ease. I couldn't wait for lunch break! I had no idea what these people were talking about.

I was required to attend meetings of Alcoholics Anonymous, Cocaine

Anonymous or Narcotics Anonymous, three to four times per week and have a sheet signed to confirm attendance at each meeting. The sheet was due at the beginning of the following week indicating compliance with the program. It would be a good idea, they said, to go with someone to my first meeting. I listened to one guy in group speak about this being his second time in recovery and he planned to get it right this time. He was an admitted alcoholic, and had been sober for about a year prior to his most recent relapse. He appeared to be humble and non threatening, so I asked if I could go to a meeting with him. He was going to an 8 p.m. meeting the next night, and wrote his phone number in the meeting schedule book that I was given.

I chain smoked Marlboros all the way to my mom's house after we were dismissed. The cigarettes worked better than the Neurontin. The longer I didn't smoke any rock the more I obsessed about it. I made sure not to drive by places where I could cop on my way back to the eastside, and white knuckled it all the way back. My mother cooked something for me when I arrived. The smell made me nauseous, but I prepared a small plate and took it to the basement. I forced myself to eat a couple of bites, and then deposited the rest in the trash. As great a cook as my mother was, I couldn't eat anything without gagging.

That evening I scraped up a buck and a half to buy a Schlitz tall boy. I took four Tylenol PMs, killed the beer, and passed out until the next day. I came-to with one of those spacy "sleeping pill hangovers." It was Tuesday and I had to call that guy about the meeting. He said I should meet him at a meeting on Broadview Road at 8 p.m., the address was already in my schedule book. I felt like I was moving in slow motion, and it was all I could do to walk upstairs from the basement. I had to get something to wake up or I would surely miss this meeting, which was on the westside! I asked my mom for money to buy coffee, and told her I was going to an A.A. meeting. A look of hope flashed across her face as she gave me the money. I drove down to East 105th and found a dope boy that pinched off a crumb for five bucks. I smoked it. That familiar smell and buzz woke me up immediately. I drove to the meeting and got there a little after 8 p.m.

I sat in my car in the parking lot across from the meeting, and stared at the meeting door for a bit. I then scraped my pipe so I could get a couple more hits out of it. It was getting later and later and I knew I had to get into that meeting, but I felt like I was stuck to the seat. I counted to 10, took a deep breath, got out and walked across the street. I stood in front of the meeting door physically shaking, paranoid, and gripped with fear not knowing what to expect. I counted to 10 again then flung open the door. A million white faces turned to look at me standing in the doorway. I wanted to turn and run, but my feet wouldn't move. This must be what a deer feels like when caught in headlights. A disembodied voice said: "Are you coming in or you just gonna stand there?" I scanned the room and saw the guy from outpatient that I was supposed to meet. I walked the seemingly 20 miles to get to his table with my head down the entire way. That was my first meeting.

CHAPTER EIGHT

Denial

I WENT BACK to outpatient the next day and they conducted a urine test. It came up dirty.

"At least I went to a meeting!" I whined.

"That's not enough; you have to stay clean too." I was put on a probationary period which meant that if I came up dirty again, I'd be dismissed from the program. I signed the paper and went to group. They passed around a sheet asking everyone to match a coping skill listed with what they saw in another client. For example, a participant matched rationalization with the woman sitting next to me. He stated that all she did was give reasons for why she drank (kids, husband, etc.), and say that she didn't really have a problem with drinking; she could stop just like she had before. My peers in the group thought that two coping skills that fit me best: denial and blame. Their acronym for denial: **Don't Even kNow I'm A Liar.** In their collective opinion, I justified my use by blaming my wife, the police, the judge; everyone except myself.

"You're all full of shit – you don't know me," I snapped. But they saw right through me.

I went to another A.A. meeting that evening by myself. It turned out to be a discussion meeting at a church on Fairmount Boulevard and attendees were a combination of older folks and people in their twenties. I sat there daring anyone to talk to me. I had nothing to say and waited to have my paper signed. *These people are drunks*, I thought, *not a dope fiend like me.* I did, however make it through the night without smoking any rock. I went home after the meeting and once again hit my mom up for a five. I left and bought a six of Gennie Cream, drank them and crashed. I was really trying not to use. Knowing that alcohol dissipated in the bloodstream more quickly than crack, heroin, and weed I felt confident that I could pass any pop up piss test if I stuck to beer. I had to have something to take the edge off nightly. It was all I could do to get through the day without picking up.

Thursday I went to a Narcotics Anonymous meeting on East 105th. It was down the street from where I would cop heroin from. Another discussion, but this meeting was hardcore. The participants were all black and these cats *looked* like dope fiends! They spoke about the disease of addiction being all inclusive. Any mood or mind altering substance qualified. I listened to guys talk about addiction and feelings, and started to identify right off the bat. The discussion went around the room until it was my turn to speak. I opened my mouth for the first time at a meeting. saying something about drinking so that I didn't use. I was immediately shouted down. I learned later that N.A. meetings were anal about there not being any mention of alcohol. It had something to do with the primary purpose of the group. Perhaps it was their way of getting back at A.A. for not allowing discussions pertaining to drugs at their meetings. Either way I was embarrassed and walked out (after my paper was signed, of course). I had enough change for a tall boy. I bought it, went to my mom's, took the last of the Tylenol PMs, and crashed.

After Friday's outpatient class, I went back to my mom's and looked around for stuff to sell so I could have some money to cop. My mother was not home when I arrived. I searched her room and closet, and found a silver brush set in a bottom drawer. I took it along with one of my acoustic guitars to a pawn shop on Euclid Avenue. I got about 40 bucks and copped two for thirty. I was sure that if I stopped using on Saturday, that would be enough time to have all the crack out of my system by Monday if they decided to test me. *Sounds good.* I was off and running again for two days.

On Saturday I received a $1,700 check from my 401(k), as I'd filled out the paperwork for it months before. I went to the bank and was able to draw approximately $100. I wanted to cash the entire amount, but the bank said I'd have to wait until it cleared the following week. There was $5 in the account at the time so I was happy that they gave me anything at all! I bought some Marlboros, gas and crack, in that order. I told myself that I would have to smoke all the rock by Saturday night because I'd need to allow enough time for it to get out of my system in case they tested me on Monday. In reality, a day is not long enough to test clean. More rationalization on my part.

I smoked that afternoon and well into the early hours of Sunday morning. The sun was rising and my heart felt like it was going to pound itself out of my chest! I was sitting on a couch in my mother's basement trying to force myself to sleep. I closed my eyes but they wouldn't stay closed. I heard every creak in the house and my fingers were black from carbon residue secondary to lighting the stem over and over again with the lighter. I felt like the living dead and I just wanted it to stop. I continued to push an antenna through the stem, pushing the makeshift pot scrubber screen (Chore Boy) so I could get another hit. *I want to go to sleep, I want another hit, I want another hit, I want to go to sleep...!*

Then I hacked up black sputum. Around noon my mother stood at the top of the stairs and asked if I wanted something to eat. I told her I'd get something later. I tried to cover my eyes with a blanket but the light of day cut through the threads of the blanket like a laser. *This sucks.* It was always the same outcome; never got better. I always went well past the "Okay, I've had enough, I'm mellow" high. Every time I got dope I told myself, *You don't have to smoke all of it.* Yet, every time I got dope, I smoked it all!

It got dark out. No sleep and my heart had slowed to a drum roll. Wide awake and tired at once. Scared to leave the basement to go upstairs for a glass of water. I started to see numbers and words written on the plaster in the basement. I saw numbers on pieces of paper and my brain told me *someone is leaving messages in code for me.* I tried to make sense of it. My paranoid mind told me it was a plot hatched by my ex to gain access to my mother's property to harm us. I believed it to be true.

Sunday night. I finally got up enough courage to sneak out of the house to buy some beer so I could get to sleep. I couldn't miss outpatient

Monday at 9 a.m., and I didn't want my mother to see me like that. I felt like I had the words, *fucked up,* stamped across my forehead. I crept upstairs, made sure the security alarm was off, opened the door to the garage slowly and closed it just as slowly. I put my car in neutral, pushed it out of the garage and started it in the driveway. I made it to CVS, bought a twelve, took it to the car, opened one and downed it. I felt a little better. I cracked open another and drove back to my mom's. I pulled into the driveway, threw the empty in the backseat, swung open the house door, slammed it shut and went to the basement with the remaining beer. *It's all okay now... I'm cool... no worries... a few more beers and I'll crash.* And eventually, I passed out.

Up all night Wednesday. I went to the bank on Thursday, got more money, then went to Record Rev for a detox kit. I could afford heroin to help bring me down. I copped some rock and heroin. I knew I had to go to a meeting; not so much for me, but to get my paper signed. I snorted some heroin and took a hit of rock. That was the high that I most enjoyed. I did one drug to counteract the other. The speedy effect of the crack had to be mellowed by the heroin. I was a good chemist.

I couldn't start nodding out in the car, so I smoked more crack to wake up. Then I got too jittery and had to snort more dog food to mellow out again. A real rollercoaster ride! I may have made it to a meeting that night. I knew that I wanted to show the folks at outpatient that I went to a meeting, plus I had to make one up for the previous week. I snorted the rest of the heroin and nodded out for the evening.

I woke up Friday morning and the dope was gone. I had an opiate buzz going so I felt no pain. I drank the detox stuff and waited to urinate before leaving for Metro. I got to Metro and tried to "act clean." My eyes were glazed and pupils dilated so any acting was to convince me more than anyone else. They didn't test me!

It was Friday and the weekend was ahead. I had enough money in the bank to buy more dope. I smoked and snorted all weekend. I was still seeing numbers everywhere: on the floor, the walls in the bathroom and on pieces of paper I'd collected in the basement and in my car. By Monday morning, I was out of my head. I was driving to Metro, when I found a dope boy to cop. I had $5. It was raining. He got into my car and took a baggie full of rocks out of his sock. He pinched off a piece for me, and got out of the car. I started to drive away when I glanced down on the passenger side floor. He had left his bag of rocks! I didn't stop driving; I ducked down, swept the bag off the floor, and kept rollin'.

I stuffed dope in my stem and smoked while driving. All of a sudden I had a brilliant thought: *I should take these papers with the numbers on them to the U.S. Marshals office and show them that my wife is trying to set me up. Then they'll arrest her and bring her to Cleveland.* This was my best thinking. I parked off East 9th, where there was construction in progress. I took my stem with me, and on my way to the Federal building I placed it in a trash can. (Not to throw it away but so I could get it when I came out.) I went into the U.S. Marshals office with my papers, and told two officers the story about how my wife was trying to set me up, and they should read the numbers and words on these pieces of paper. They looked at each other, looked at the papers, looked at me and then at one another again.

"We don't see anything on here. Why don't you take these to the FBI. They have a powerful microscope that could probably see the words and numbers," they said smirking at each other. I thanked them for their help, asked which way to the FBI building and took off.

On my way to East 9th I remembered I was supposed to be at outpatient. I was on a mission though! I stopped at the car and took out my outpatient folder which had the direct phone number, and decided to call after speaking with the FBI. I went into the Federal Bureau of Investigation and told them that the Marshals office sent me. I wanted to know if they could see the numbers and words on my papers with one of their high powered microscopes. The agents took my papers, asked for my phone number and said they would call with the results. I was relieved and thanked them.

I still haven't heard from them.

I went to a phone booth outside and called Metro to let them know that I would be late because I was ill. I walked to the trash can and rummaged around until I found my stem. When I arrived at outpatient, they wanted to piss test me. I gave them some urine, went to group and waited. My counselor called me into his office and told me that I'd been using. I made a feeble attempt at lying but even I knew it was no use.

"You must have just used because the particles in the pee sample haven't even broken down yet," he said. "I'm sorry, but you have to leave. Your best bet will be to go to an inpatient facility." He gave me a list of about five inpatient treatment centers and wished me luck.

I WAS NOT too broken up about being kicked out of outpatient. After all, I still had the dope the guy left in my car. I took a hit in the parking lot and drove back to my mom's to smoke the rest. Same story: up all night and wanted more. Living with myself was becoming more and more unbearable. I missed my girls. My oldest daughter's birthday was coming and I was out of money again. I asked my mother for money to buy her a birthday card. She sent my daughter a check from me. I felt worthless. I got a card and tried to write something. It was difficult because I was geeked and crying. I don't remember what I wrote or if it made sense.

In order to stay at my mom's, I had to pretend that I was still going to outpatient at Metro on Mondays, Wednesdays, and Fridays. I started leaving the side door unlocked when I left so that I could sneak back in when my mom was out, as she had taken my key some time ago. She didn't want me in her house when she wasn't there. I knew that she would leave for Tai Chi classes during the day so I'd go in when she was gone.

I had taken some of her old books to an antiques store on Larchmere, and found a demand for some of her other items at various antique stores on the street. I started taking hats, the old Sunday church going kind, and found a demand for them at one place. The lady said: "Bring all you have." I did. I grabbed old linen and anything else I could find and sold them, including a CD player from my mom's room. She noticed things disappearing and confronted me. I told her I didn't know what she was talking about. All I did at this point was smoke. I started pawning more of my guitars. (Bass guitarist Dave Valentine from I-Tal would later give me $80 to get my guitar out of pawn so we could play again once I got sober.) I knew I was on borrowed time at my mom's. I told her I was going to try inpatient treatment to which she said: "Do it now!" I started asking her for $5 every morning to get coffee. I actually needed it to get a five piece so I could function. (Later she told me that she knew why I needed $5 everyday and she was afraid of what I might do if she didn't give it to me.)

I became more and more irrational. It didn't take much for me to start yelling when I didn't get what I wanted. My mother was scared to live in her own house while I was there. I was the ultimate King Baby! I pulled out the sheet from Metro with the list of treatment centers. One of them was Freedom House on West 25th. I decided to get in there, so I drove over, smoking dope the entire way. I sat in the parking lot trying to coerce myself out of the car. I eventually went inside knowing that I still had dope in my car: *I'll go in here and tell them I'll be back later with my things.* I waited for what seemed like hours. Finally this big biker-looking cat came over.

"So you want to get clean?" he asked. I said sure. "We might have a bed open in a few days if you want to come back." I said no problem and headed to my car to smoke. I was lighting up before I pulled out of the parking lot. I smoked the rest and headed back to my mom's. I looked at the sheet again and saw a place called Orca House. I was geeked and could hardly speak, but called anyway. I told someone that I needed help because I couldn't stop smoking crack. They said a bed would be available in a week, I should come in for assessment, and be prepared to stay on April 19, 2001. They also said don't use in the meantime. *This is stupid! I just said I can't stop!* I agreed. That was a long week that got worse.

CHAPTER NINE

Smoking with the Dead

IT WAS NO LONGER about trying not to use. I had to use. I knew I would die if I continued to use and I knew I'd die if I stopped. This is what is called the "jumping off point." I didn't want to live anymore. Inpatient treatment was my last hope, provided I could make it through the week. I'd curse whatever God was out there every morning when I awoke. That meant that I would have to get through another day of finding money to cop and once I did, an endless cycle of finding money to get more dope.... Again and again and again until I either passed out, or stayed up all night. The next day the hell would start all over again.

The daily $5 from my mother was just enough to start the insanity. I was living by animal instinct: survival was my focus. I planned to strong arm a business man downtown to get money. I was sitting in my car around West 4th and Superior waiting for the right guy to walk by: someone smaller and weaker than I. Each one that walked by seemed like he could kick my ass! I planned suicide instead. Anything to stop the mental anguish and futility of my disgusting life. *I could jump off the Superior Bridge. What if I don't die and become a cripple or something? I'll have to depend on someone else to get my drugs for me.* I tried slitting my wrist once while on the road with the band in Augusta. That hurt too much, and I was afraid to slice too deeply. I made a feeble attempt at overdosing but all that happened was that I kept buying more. I couldn't even kill myself correctly.

April 19, 2001 fell on a Thursday, and I was to be there for my assessment at 1 p.m. I had gotten high every day until the evening before. I was up all night and hadn't slept. My eyes were bulging out of my head and I weighed 134 lbs. There was a sore on my tailbone because I had no butt cheeks to cushion me when sitting. I'd sit directly on the tail end of my spine, and would constantly rock back and forth to offset the pressure of sitting. I forced myself into the shower just to get water on me. I shivered uncontrollably regardless of whether the water was hot or not. I packed a small bag with dirty socks, a pair of pants and T-shirt that was in a corner, and joined my mother in the car. We stopped at the store and she bought two packs of Marlboros for me, and arrived at Orca a little before 1 p.m. My mother reached into her purse and gave me a 10 dollar bill. She looked at me and said: "Now go and do what you need to do." She looked relieved, like a burden had been lifted. I got out of her car and told her I had to smoke a cigarette before I went in because I was nervous. She told me she loved me, backed out of the driveway, turned right onto Chester Avenue from East 89th and disappeared.

I lit up a Marlboro. I looked at Orca House, looked down the street, looked at Orca once more, picked up my bag and started walking down East 89th toward Cedar Road. I got to Cedar, turned right and went down to East 79th. I had $10 in my pocket and I had to get just one more.

I copped a ten piece from a dopeboy and headed up Cedar with it in my fist, looking for something to use to smoke it. I tried to bend antennas of cars trying to break one off so I could use it as a stem. All would bend back and forth and not break. I walked up a little ways into a cut off of Cedar. There was an old couch near a tree, empty beer cans and cigarette butts all around. I scanned the area for anything I could put this rock in. I saw the plastic holder of a cigar, and dug out the butt that was left. I put the rock in there and lit it with my lighter. I heard it sizzle and pop. I was smoking crack and plastic as the holder melted in my hand. I don't know if I got off on the dope or the plastic fumes. I sat down on the funky smelling couch and scanned the ground for a piece I could have possibly dropped. All I found was the carcass of a dog that I had completely overlooked while looking for a stem. It was only a few feet from me and I didn't see it a few moments before. *I'm smoking with the dead now.*

Hopeless, demoralized and full of fear, I started the slow walk up Cedar to the only place I had left to go. I'd hoped that I didn't screw it up by walking away.

I stopped inside the newly built Cleveland Clinic Intercontinental Hotel and bummed a quarter from a guy to call Orca. I looked through the phone book to find the number. I couldn't read a thing: the numbers and words ran together. I couldn't think. I asked a hotel guest to find the number for me and he pointed it out. I put the quarter in the phone, dialed the first three numbers and forgot the next four. That happened a couple of times until I asked another guest to dial for me. When a lady answered I told her I had a 1 p.m. appointment and I would be there in a few minutes.

"We had given up on you," she said. "We saw you leave when you got here at one. Don't bother coming if you're not here in the next five minutes." She hung up. Orca was a block away from where I was. I walked to the house, up the driveway, up the front steps and stood at the large, heavy double doors. I did the old count to ten thing, took a deep breath and went into the house.

PART II

CHAPTER TEN

Orca House

I WALKED into Orca and met Midge, the one I spoke with on the phone. She escorted me into an office where I was asked to empty my pockets. I had a lighter and a pack and a half of cigarettes. Midge asked one of the monitors of the house to search my bag and then she began asking me questions which she entered into a computer.

"Have you used today?" she asked.

"Yes," I answered.

"When was the last time?"

"About twenty minutes ago."

"You're high right now?" I thought for a second before I answered. I prepared for the worst and started thinking about where I would go if they didn't let me in. I had no place to go. I had burned all of my bridges. "Didn't we tell you not to use before you got here?" she snapped. *Crap! How am I not supposed to use?! I can't stop. That's why I'm here!*

"Yes, but..."

She continued to ask questions about types of drugs I used and if I had any diseases. I couldn't think of any diseases from the top of my head but I was able to rattle off a long list of drugs. After what seemed to be a few hours she asked me to drop urine. She said everyone had to drop when they came into the house. I breathed a sigh of relief; she was going to let me stay! I was coming down from the high and starting to get anxious, shaky and fearful; all of the symptoms that usually preceded running to get high as quickly as possible. For some reason I felt that I could tell Midge how I was feeling. After all, she was letting me stay and deep down, I knew that if I didn't get clean now, I may never have another chance at it. I knew that if I left to get high that I wouldn't come back to Orca. But I wanted to get high; it was too uncomfortable trying to talk and think.

I told Midge that I didn't know if I could do this; stay there all night without something to help me sleep. I told her that if I'm not passed out then I would get overwhelmed by the urge to use. Midge told me that she was a recovered alcoholic and had been clean for more than ten years. She said she knew how I felt, and started talking to me like she cared and understood how I was feeling. This was the first time someone understood how badly I needed to get high. Not WANTED to get high, NEEDED to get high! For the first time I didn't feel so alone, as someone else knew the dread and hopelessness I felt. I told her again that I didn't know if I could stay all night without leaving to get high. There were no locks on the doors to keep clients from leaving. If you left the house you left of your own free will.

"I'm not supposed to do this but I have a few Benadryl," Midge said. "I'll give you a couple to help you sleep tonight. Don't tell anyone I gave you these 'cause I could lose my job over it. Also, I want you to ask God to take the taste out of your mouth." The Benadryl, I thought, would help more than asking God to do anything for me but I said it anyway.

"God, please take the taste of drugs and alcohol out of my mouth."

Midge paged one of the 15 clients in the house. She asked him which room had a bed available, and to show me the way. I went up the front stairway, and into the room. It had two other client beds in there. All sorts of thoughts were running through my head: *Will these guys like me? Will I be able to sleep in this place? What if I get into a fight?* The house rules were given to me. I was supposed to go over it, sign the sheet stating that I understood, and return it to Midge. Mostly everyone was downstairs at this time; clients were not permitted upstairs during treatment hours which ended around 4:30. It was right before dinner and everyone was watching TV. My name was now...The New Guy.

Someone started screaming: "Chow time, chow time!" Someone else said: "Go get the new guy!" I went downstairs and 15 dudes were standing in line in front of the half door leading to the kitchen with empty plates in their hands. I was at the end of the line which was okay because I wasn't hungry. They were serving liver and onions! I hated liver, and hadn't eaten it since a babysitter forced it down my throat when I was five. We took our plates to the dining room which held four large folding tables and folding chairs. We had to stand while someone said a prayer before we could sit to eat. I was not feeling all this prayer stuff! We sat and began to eat. I gave my liver to the guy next to me and he immediately made a loud comment to everyone: "The new guy just gave me his plate of food!" *Oh crap...what did I do now?* Others chimed in: "Oh, you ain't hungry? You better eat this shit...you'll be hungry later!" *Maybe so, but I'm not hungry now!*

After dinner, every man took his plate into the kitchen, scraped off the residual food and placed it in the sink. The dishes had to be washed and dried before we could leave for our nightly 7:30 meeting. Plus the house rules were read every Thursday before leaving for the meeting. A light-skinned, muscular brother with corn rows was rinsing off the dishes and swearing at the guys who had left food on their plates. This cat looked like he just stepped out of the joint! I found out later he was brought there by the sheriff department in handcuffs and leg irons.

He yelled: "Who's gonna help me with these fucking dishes?!" Guess who? ...The New Guy! This was my first chore at the house. Everyone had a chore which included mopping on weekends, cleaning the toilets and cooking. I was dumbfounded. I didn't wash and dry dishes at home let alone for 15 guys! The guy's name was Malik, and he showed me what to do. Before I knew it I was washing those nasty dishes. I wound up doing kitchen duty for two months.

Malik asked me what was my drug of choice. I told him crack and heroin. He told me he was a crack-a-holic. I could identify with that and we became friends. We were called into the living room for House Rules.

Tyrone E. was the monitor for the evening. He was missing a few teeth and liked to chew gum. Whenever he talked, I focused on the gum in his mouth, wondering how he kept it from flying out. He started reading from the same sheet Midge had given me earlier: "No smoking in the house, no swearing, clients are expected to make their beds every morning...." Then all of a sudden he says, "and there's no bumping dickheads in the shower...save that shit for when you leave here!" *What?! Did I hear that right?! I don't remember seeing that!*

After the rules and regs were read, we went across the street to a church basement where there was a Cocaine Anonymous meeting. We walked in. There were a bunch of people talking and laughing, introducing themselves and trying to hug me. This made me very uncomfortable (especially after hearing about dickheads in the shower)! They said: "We don't shake hands here, we hug!" The last thing I wanted was for anyone to talk to me let alone hug me. A guy came over and handed me five raffle tickets. I told him that I didn't have any money but he insisted: "They're for you." *Right... And what do you expect from me?* I kept my eye on this cat. Everybody was too damned nice and happy. I didn't trust a single one of them. Tyrone, the house monitor, said: "Let us love you until you learn to love yourself." I was trusting them even less.

We sat down and the meeting started. There were three people sitting at a table. One stood up and started a reading about being an addict that caught my attention. The reader said something about not being able to live or breathe without cocaine, and I could identify with that. They finished the readings and introduced the lady sitting at the table. She stood up and said: "Hi family, my name is Valerie and I'm an addict." Everybody responded with: "Hi Valerie!" She went on: "God, grant me the serenity to accept the things I cannot change, the courage to change the things I can, and the wisdom to know the difference." Little did I know at that time I would recite this prayer often!

Valerie talked about drinking and snorting cocaine, then smoking coke and being homeless. I could identify with this, too. When she started talking about getting clean, however, she completely lost me. I had heard something about the twelve steps before but now this woman was explaining every one. I looked at the clock. *Will this shit ever end?!* I stopped hearing anything, and began to shift around in my seat. I complained to the guy next to me, and someone behind me said: "Shhh, one meeting, please!" Not only was I restless, now I was pissed! *When is this chick gonna sit down?!* Finally, she stopped talking and sat down. *Thank God, now we can go.* They invited people to comment. *I can't believe this! How much longer?!* It seemed like everybody in the room had something to say. Just as I thought they were done, another one popped up and started his endless opinion. Finally, one of the guys at the desk asked: "Are there any further comments?" I was evil eyeing and daring anyone else to stand up. *Thank goodness...no more comments.* The guy at the table said: "I'd like to thank everyone for their comments." *Now we can get this show on the road and leave...what the fuck?!* HE started to comment. *Just shut up already!*

"I now pass it over to the secretary." Another guy started talking. *What could possibly be left to say?! Oh my God! If I had a gun, I'd make a comment!* Announcements were read. *Can we go, please?! Oh great...now there's a fucking raffle! Whoever has #702...?*

"702...702 going once? Twice?" He pulled another number. "812? Anybody have 812?" Some dude walked up to claim his $5, and I saw the guy who gave me the tickets. I handed him back his tickets and said thanks anyway. He looked at them. "You had 702!"

"No way," I said.

"Yes you do. It's the last three numbers on the ticket, not the first three!" *Crap!*

Later I stopped Tyrone the monitor.

"How often do we have to go to these meetings?" I asked.

"Everyday," he replied. *Just shoot me, NOW!*

We went back across the street to Orca House, and somebody screamed: "Snack time! Go show the new guy how to get snacks." The peer leader grabbed my arm and took me to the basement. We went into what looked like a root cellar, where there were five Tupperware bins stacked by a wall. He opened the bins containing every type of junk food imaginable. He started picking.

"Some of these... a couple of these... gotta have this." We went back upstairs arms full of cookies, Little Debbies and candy bars. We put them on the table, and the guys started grabbing them. One guy said: "Who got these cookies?" The peer leader responded: "The new dude!" The client clicked his tongue. "New dude...these things *suck!* Next time do a better job!" I started pouting and swearing under my breath. I refused to eat any of it.

Tyrone the monitor came over to me and asked me if I wanted to get sober. I told him I'd tried before but it didn't work. While the guys were inhaling the snacks, Tyrone and I sat at his desk by the main entrance and talked. He told me he was a heroin addict too and had been clean for about eight years. He told me about stuff he did on the streets when he was caught up in active addiction. It all sounded familiar. There were a couple of things he did that I'd sworn I would never do.

"Never say never," he said. "That's just a YET for you. If you want the drug badly enough you'll do anything to get it. Take a look at your life to see when you did things for dope that you swore you'd never do." I remembered when I first started smoking weed, I said I would never touch coke or heroin. Eventually I did both. Tyrone said that the acronym YET means: You're Eligible Too.

I asked him how he got clean, and he said that the first thing he had to do was to stop fighting and surrender. I had to admit to my innermost self that I had no power over drugs and alcohol.

"Well, I stopped before but then I started again," I said.

"It's not about stopping; it's about *not starting*. If you're on a train track and you get hit by a train, it's not the caboose that kills you; it's the engine!" I ran that through what was left of my mind.

"So if I don't start then I don't have to stop, right?" He agreed. Now a couple of remaining brain cells fired.

"But if I'm powerless over dope and alcohol, how the hell do I not start?" I knew I had him now!

"You have to find a power greater than yourself that will solve your problem." I could see how dope had dictated my every move, so I knew there was definitely a power greater than me. I could also see how I would continue to drink when I'd swear I'd just have one or that I wouldn't drink at all for the evening. Eventually, I continued to drink when I didn't even want or plan to. There had to be a power greater than Jose Cuervo and Heineken. I was no different from people who could control their alcohol intake. Then again, if *I* can't stop, then I *must* be different.

This was a moment of clarity for me. I had always wondered how some people could go into a bar, order one beer, drink half of it and leave! I never left half a beer unless I had passed out. If I ever had one beer and left the bar, you could be sure that I had more at home or I went to another bar. And there were times when I'd go into a panic because it was getting close to 2 a.m. and I had to run out of the house to make sure I had enough to drink for the rest of the evening. I don't believe "normal" drinkers risked life and limb to get to the beer store before it closed.

I was comfortable talking to Tyrone and I wanted to keep talking to find out how he'd gotten clean. I had a tiny, tiny thought in the back of my head: *If he can do it, why not me?* Tyrone told me it was lights out and I would have to go to my room, as there was therapeutic walk at 5 a.m. I told him I wouldn't be able to sleep. He told me to rest anyway. It then occurred to me that I had a couple of Benadryl!

"Good night, Tyrone." I went upstairs. *What the hell is a therapeutic walk?*

CHAPTER ELEVEN

Difficult to Escape Me

I WAS AWAKENED abruptly by some dude screaming in my room: "This is not the Holiday Inn! Therapeutic walk time!"

It's 5 a.m. The Benadryl did the job and I actually got some sleep. At least enough that I would have preferred to stay in bed a bit longer. My two roommates jumped out of bed and said: "New dude....get up!" They were both on their knees next to their beds, and it looked like they were praying! One of these cats was about 6'4", built like the Hulk and just released from prison. I figured that I was the one that should have been praying 'cause he was my roommate! His name was Eric. He stood up to make his bed while singing, "We fall down but we get up," in a fantastic baritone voice! Everyone in the house was scrambling for the showers. I learned that if you didn't get in the shower early, you were out of luck regarding hot water. I made sure I was the last and only person in the shower; Tyrone's line about bumping dickheads still disturbed me!

I was freezing from the cold water; it was a quick shower. The second floor had three rooms for clients. There were three beds in my room, two beds in the room across the hall, and five beds in the room down the hall (two bunkbeds and a single). The third floor had a separate shower and bathroom with a total of six beds. We were all expected downstairs at 6 a.m., and we gathered outside. Most of us lit up cigarettes to prepare for the walk. The house monitor asked one of the peer leaders to check the house for stragglers and then did a head count. Everybody was present and we began to walk down Chester Avenue.

It was cold enough for me to see my breath. We started out together but before long clients walked in little groups. I was at the back of the pack by myself, semi-trying to keep up. Someone shouted: "Come on new dude!" The monitor fell back to walk with me. I was already tired and we hadn't even walked a block. I was still feeling dope sick from not having any methadone or heroin for awhile. Queasy stomach, back pain, nose running...feeling crappy. Man, I was out of shape! The monitor and I started talking. He was a recovered addict. I told him how my wife left me and how much I missed my kids, and that I'd never see any of them again.

"The main thing you should concern yourself with is getting and staying clean and sober. You have to do it for yourself. This is the selfish part of the program. You have to get clean for you; not your mother, wife, kids or anyone else," he said. I couldn't understand that. I wanted to get clean *so* I could see my kids again and be a better father. Wasn't that what a good man was supposed to do? Take care of his wife and kids? "How can you take care of someone else when you can't take care of yourself right now?" he asked. It was the truth, but I didn't want to hear it. It hurt. "If you get clean for your wife, what happens if she doesn't want to be with you? Then, your reason for staying clean is gone. What if you get clean for your mother? She won't be around forever and when she passes, your reason for being clean is gone...might as well get high. What if your kids get mad at you, refuse to see you, or maybe you won't see them again... what then?"

"Then my reason for staying clean is gone, right?"

He nodded. "Get sober for you and only you. The ability to have decent relationships with others is a by-product of recovery and not the purpose." I told him that I was afraid my wife was cheating on me. I kept thinking about it and saying it over and over again to the point of driving myself crazy. Now that I didn't have any dope in me to cover up my feelings they all came crashing to the forefront of my mind: my insecurities fueled my anxiety. Eric, my roommate, overheard me whining and gave me some wisdom that would stick with me.

"You don't control your wife's legs...she can open them to anyone she wants to." That shit hurt! Everything I heard that rang of truth hurt like hell. "We don't sugarcoat shit here!" he said.

We made it back to the house and I felt as though I'd been through an emotional wringer. I wanted to go to bed and pull the covers over my head but instead was forced to be with 15 other guys. It was becoming difficult to escape me. We stood before the dining room tables for breakfast and Eric said a prayer. I sat at a long table with the guys, but felt alone even though I was surrounded. They were making toast and passing sausage, and I sat there, numb. I wanted to leave. I wanted to get away physically and mentally. I didn't know it at the time but this was my first introduction to facing life without the use of mind-altering substances. It sucked!

After breakfast I washed the dishes. Still numb, I thought about my wife and kids. *Where are they? What are they doing? Do they still care about me?* I finished the dishes, and we gathered at the tables in the dining room for morning meditation. One of us read aloud from the 24 Hour A Day meditation book while everyone else followed along. After the reading, we took turns commenting on what was read. The reading for April 20, 2001 (the first whole day that I would be drug and alcohol free):

A.A. THOUGHT FOR THE DAY

"The satisfaction you get out of living a sober life is made up of a lot of little things, but they add up to a satisfactory and happy life. You take out of life what you put into it. So I'd say to people coming into A.A.: 'Don't worry about what life will be like without liquor. Just hang in there and a lot of good things will happen to you. And you'll have that feeling of quiet satisfaction and peace and serenity and gratitude for the grace of God.' Is my life really becoming worth living?"

The morning readings became a guiding hand. Many times I would spend the evening worrying about my life and future and the reading for the next day would either answer my questions or calm me enough to get through another day. I was starting to see a higher power working in my life but I was not ready to acknowledge it yet. It had to be coincidence.

After we were done with comments we said the Lord's Prayer (which I didn't know), had a 10-minute cigarette break, then went back inside for group therapy. In group we learned about the disease of addiction and were introduced to a number of tools to assist with delving deeper into ourselves. This was the first time I sat still long enough to focus on what was going on inside me. I had known all along that I wouldn't like what I would find so I never really had incentive to look. Besides, all of my problems were because of someone or something other than me! If my wife hadn't left me I wouldn't have to get high. If she hadn't taken my daughters then I could stop drinking and doing drugs. If all my so-called friends really cared about me then I wouldn't be here. If the police gave me a break instead of always locking me up maybe I'd have a chance to do the right thing. If the judge would believe me instead of taking my wife's side...and on and on.

They talked about a tool, Jahari's window, that demonstrated how we saw ourselves and the way others saw us. I found there to be a great divide between the two. We were introduced to a pamphlet, King Baby, which dealt with self centeredness and self obsession. It seemed to describe me. I began to see that although I talked about my concerns regarding my wife, children and mother, I was concerned more with how I believed their actions affected me rather than how they were affected by my actions. I was full of anger, resentment and fear. We were charged with writing a biography about ourselves and to be prepared to read it aloud to our peers in two weeks. *Great, homework. That's alright 'cause I've got plenty of shit to tell these assholes!*

After group we had a cigarette break before lunch, and after lunch, another cigarette break before a different group. Of course I had to finish washing dishes before I could smoke. I usually had enough time to smoke half of one and save the rest for later. This next group was facilitated by a guy that was a hardcore recovered addict. He was in N.A. and had a take-no-shit attitude. He introduced me to the Hot Seat. A client sat in the center of a circle of his peers, and the facilitator would ask those in the surrounding circle to tell the person in the Hot Seat what they don't like about him.

My brain was doing somersaults thinking about being called into the circle. I watched guys in the Hot Seat get pissed off one minute to almost in tears the next! The client in the Hot Seat was supposed to sit and listen to the comments but that rarely happened. Chairs were thrown occasionally along with the use of colorful language. The facilitator deliberately said things to piss off the guy in the center. Just when the person in the center wanted to kill the facilitator he said: "Now, see how easy it is to have someone knock you off your square?" He continued, "What if your wife or girlfriend pisses you off? Or your boss? What are you going to do then? You can either learn to control your reactions or your reactions will control you!" It was about *responding* instead of reacting to situations.

My first reaction to anything I perceived to be a threat to my self-esteem was violent and often irrational. Anything to show the other person that I was not weak and deserved respect. The less self-esteem I had, the more volatile my reaction to the "threat" to my masculinity. The facilitator asked us to take a look at how we felt before we blew up.

"We all feel something before we react or respond. The trick is to take the time to recognize the feeling before reacting. That millisecond of self evaluation is long enough to make a thoughtful response instead of an instant reaction." Instant reactions usually got me in trouble one way or another. My emotions were raw anyway. I wondered how anyone could live in this world and take the shit it dishes out without some sort of pill or beer to take the edge off: a 5 mg Valium or *something*. I no longer had the option to use anymore unless, of course, I wanted more of what got me to Orca House in the first place. I had to learn new ways of dealing with life, as my way simply didn't work anymore.

I felt like using daily for the first couple of weeks at Orca. I was advised by the house monitors and people at meetings to "tell on my disease." Meaning, we should tell someone when we felt like using. If we kept that knowledge to ourselves, we may have acted on it. The whole thing about telling people how I felt was scary. I didn't want another man to know how I felt, as I couldn't let my guard down. I couldn't let those cats think I was a punk or weak! I confided to Tyrone the monitor what I thought about telling another man my business.

"You can't save your ass and your face at the same time!" Tyrone always had some slick words of recovery to share. He told me that it was time for me to start asking for and using the help that was around me. "A closed mouth don't get fed. What happened when you tried to get clean and sober all those times alone?"

"It didn't work. Eventually I got high again."

"Then why not try something different this time? Take a chance and try something new!"

I smirked. "I still can't tell anyone my business."

"You ain't got no business in here!" Followed by another thought provoking tip: "Your mind is like a parachute... it works best when it's open!" *Where does he get this shit?!*

CHAPTER TWELVE

Hope

ONCE THE BENADRYL was gone, I did not sleep well. I complained to a counselor, hoping they would give me something to help me sleep. My counselor told me that no one ever died from lack of sleep and that eventually I'd start sleeping. Wasn't the answer I wanted to hear. It was Saturday morning, my third day without drugs and alcohol. *Man, if this is sobriety, I don't want it!* I felt miserable, like I was going to jump out of my skin. Every time I heard someone open a can of pop my mind immediately jumped to the thought of a beer being opened. If I saw someone flick a lighter, my mind flashed to lighting a stem full of crack. I was bugging out. I mention this to Tyrone; hearing and seeing these things were a trigger for me to use.

"A trigger don't mean nothing if the gun ain't loaded!" he quipped. I didn't understand. Until the obsession to use had been lifted, he said, I was still suffering from untreated alcoholism. A trigger was nothing but an excuse to use. My sponsor would later tell me that a "trigger ain't nothing but Roy Rogers' horse and they're both dead!" *How do I get rid of this obsession to use?*

Saturday mornings consisted of a therapeutic walk, cereal for breakfast, then doing chores. Hot food was cooked for breakfast during the week and we had cold food on the weekends. I ate Lucky Charms mostly on weekends. Chores for the weekend included mopping the floors and stairs, and scrubbing the toilets in the bathrooms. I was mopping floors, washing dishes, making my bed and cleaning toilets! I rarely (if at all) did this when I had a home and family let alone for a bunch of dudes! I didn't know it at the time but I was being taught to be responsible and more importantly to GROW UP!

The thoughts of using kept at me, especially when I had to do something against my will. This time I told the weekend monitor what I was feeling. He suggested I say the Serenity Prayer. *Great. Another prayer I have to learn along with the Lord's Prayer.* He told me that he said the prayer over and over again early in his sobriety and it helped him get through the rough spots. I copied the Serenity Prayer onto a piece of paper and kept it in my pocket. I brought it out and read it whenever I was buggin' out, which seemed to be quite often.

A phone hung on the wall in the reception area that we were allowed to use occasionally affectionately known as "the relapse box." Guys would get on the phone in an attempt to control things at home: their girlfriends, wives, or anything that made them feel as though they had some power. Tyrone would say: "If you're not working on recovery, you're working on a relapse." Guys screamed and swore into the phone. Some would freak out having supposedly heard another man's voice in the background. A few packed up and left because they had to see what was going on at home. We were easily distracted when it came to sitting still and looking at ourselves.

I opened up a little to some of the guys in the house, as I began to realize that I wasn't as unique as I'd thought. Each had his own story about how he got there. Some were trying to get sober. Some were on paper and others were simply trying to stay out of jail. One guy told me: "The judge gave me the option one time to go to treatment for 90 days with one year probation or jail time. I took the jail time 'cause I didn't want to be on paper and I knew I couldn't stay clean that long. This time I have to be here 'cause the judge was talking about putting me away for a few years if I didn't go to treatment."

During down time, after meetings before lights out, clients played cards, dominoes or watched TV. I spent most of my time working out in the makeshift weight room, as I found that working out helped to take focus off of using, at least for a short time. I still felt queasy and nauseous daily. The weight room was on the third floor, so I was fairly secluded up there; I needed to be away from all those dudes sometimes.

I met a guy in the weight room who would later become my best friend, sponsee and only brother I'd ever known. Tyrone S. was a skinny guy who came to the house a month before I had arrived. He went up to the weight room not to workout but to iron his pants. We began talking and found out that we had some things in common. One being a heroin and crack habit and the other was having a daughter about the same age. We began to meet in the weight room and talk about our kids and family.

"My oldest daughter, who was eight years old, begged me not to leave the house one night," I told him. "I had been leaving every evening to score dope. Sometimes I wouldn't come back until the next day. My daughter wanted me to stay home just one night. I promised her that night that I would. With everything in me I told myself I would not leave the house that evening and I meant it. I had never broken a promise to my little girl. The hours crept by, and with each passing minute, I told myself to stay put. I was restless and irritable. I began pacing around the house. Finally I told my daughter I'd be right back. She screamed, 'You promised!' I said 'I promise I'll be right back!' I could see the tears in her eyes as I walked out the door. I didn't come back until early the next morning and then I went directly to the basement to smoke. My wife would comfort my daughter while I was gone."

We also talked a lot about what was required to stay clean and sober. A counselor told us once that only two out of 16 would stay sober. That night in the weight room, when everyone else was watching basketball or playing cards, Tyrone and I agreed that we would be those two. We talked about how hopeless and worthless we felt; like we weren't any use to ourselves or others. We talked about how we hurt the people we loved most: our children, parents, wives, anyone who cared about us. We talked about how we both wanted and tried to stop using and couldn't no matter what.

Sundays were pretty laid back. Some of the guys who had been at the house longer were permitted to go to church. Everyone else attended a men's discussion meeting from 10 a.m. until noon. Three topics were chosen and everyone participated in the discussion. This was the first time I saw some old timers in recovery. Some of these guys had more than 30 years sober which I couldn't comprehend. I had trouble staying clean for 30 minutes at a time let alone 30 years! I asked one these cats how he stayed sober for such a long time. He told me: "I only have to stay sober a day at a time. It's too difficult to try to stay sober for the rest of my life. All we have is today."

That was the same thing I was told when I first got there and wanted to use. They said: "Just don't use for a minute...and when that minute's over don't use for the next minute...and when that minute is over don't use for the next one." The minutes added up to hours and before I knew it, it would be morning and time to get up. Another recovered alcoholic would later share: "It's hard by the yard but a cinch by the inch!"

Sunday was also the day when family members would visit. By afternoon, the house would be full of visitors ranging from infants to the elderly coming to support their loved one in treatment. Before family was allowed visitation they were required to attend a family night to learn about the disease of addiction. The only family that came for me was my mother; no friends, children, wife, brothers or sisters. It actually took about three weeks before my mother visited for the first time. I was surprised that she came at all, after the crap I put her through. She would later tell me that she knew there was no one else to visit me, as I had successfully destroyed or isolated myself from all relationships. I don't remember Tyrone S. having many, if anyone, visit either. We both had burned many bridges.

I recalled my last months before entering treatment. The loneliness was unbearable. I'd think about the happy times... when my first daughter was born, when my second daughter was born and how I missed them hugging me and calling me Daddy. I remembered how, with my mother's help, we were able to purchase our first home, and when my wife's family would visit on holidays with presents for the girls. There was a time when

I had a family that loved me and now they were disgusted with me. All the alcohol and dope in the city couldn't fully erase that feeling of loneliness and despair, but it did take the edge off momentarily. Now I had to learn how to deal with those feelings without using.

We walked to a meeting on East 105th after dinner. I was thinking about all the family that showed for the other guys and no one for me. I felt sorry for myself, and shared my thoughts with Tyrone S. He reminded me that things weren't always about us; other people had lives too. He went on to say that we had done a lot of damage and couldn't expect the world to always go the way we wanted it to.

"You weren't thinking about your family when you would stay out all night getting high, were you?" he asked.

I hadn't a clue where my wife and children were anyway. Being at the meeting that evening dispelled some of my loneliness and self-pity. I knew that being around recovered addicts gave me a feeling of togetherness; a common bond. I recognized that I wasn't the only one feeling lonely, that others felt the same way, but were able to get through the feelings without picking up a drink or drug in order to cope. They used the power of the group: "A problem shared is a problem cut in half." After hearing the speaker that evening my problems seemed miniscule compared to his, and he didn't pick up. I started to identify with the feelings instead of judging the messengers. For the first time I began to feel "a part of" and not separate. The name of the meeting: WE ARE FAMILY!

After the Sunday night meeting, I felt okay, that everything was going to be alright. Before going to bed I knelt down next to it and said three words: "Please help me." I didn't know to whom or what I was saying this but I gave it a try. What did I have to lose?

Monday morning started like the previous weekdays. Up early for therapeutic walk, breakfast and morning meditation from the 24 Hour a Day book. I talked to the monitor on the walk and told him that I had a feeling that everything was going to be alright.

"It'll be alright as long as you don't pick up. Right now you're on a 'pink cloud.' Enjoy it while it lasts," he said. The pink cloud experience happens to most of us early in sobriety. It is when we begin to have hope that there is a future for ourselves. I could now label my first true feeling while sober: hope.

CHAPTER THIRTEEN

Meadowbrook Road

AS THE DAYS went by, I paid more attention to what the counselors were saying. I asked questions, watched the Orca House alumni and the clean and sober people that ran meetings, and talked to us about sobriety.

One day my mother forwarded a letter to me from an attorney regarding the reselling of our most recent home which we were planning to buy once it was out of probate. The court advised my wife and I that we no longer had an option to purchase the home. Having spent all of the money we were going to use to apply toward the purchase, being separated from my wife, and currently residing in a treatment center, I could certainly see their point!

The letter advised us to remove any remaining property from the home or it would be put on the street. The only things left in the house were an old day bed, my grandmother's large console stereo, an old color TV, a freezer my mother gave us and a house full of memories. My wife had taken all of the furniture and anything of value, along with our daughters, with her. There was also a snow blower in the garage that didn't have a key.

I began to panic and kept rereading the letter to figure out what to do. I had fallen off of my pink cloud. Fear and anxiety leapt in. *What am I going to do? How am I going to get this stuff and where am I going to put it?* I didn't want to lose the only material things I had left. I told my new friend Tyrone S. about the problem. He suggested I talk to my counselor about it. *Gee, never thought of that.* I went to my counselor, Jennie, a former client at Orca Women's House, now sober and working at the men's house. I had talked to her about my kids and wife so she knew my family history and situation.

"Is that stuff really important to you?"

"It's all I have," I said.

Looking back at it, I was trying to hold onto memories and whatever was left in the house, even if it was worthless. I asked her if I could go there to prepare the things that needed to be moved.

"I trust you," she said.

All I wanted to do was learn how to stay sober, but I was dragged back to the responsibilities of cleaning up the wreckage of my past. This was overwhelming. I was shaky with my limited "so*dry*ety" when I found myself taking a bus to my old house. I said the Serenity Prayer on the bus, and told myself that I would just get those things ready to be moved and return to Orca.

I walked down Meadowbrook Road to the house from the bus stop and stood in front looking at it. Memories flooded in. Feelings that I had been trying to deal with began to deal with me instead. My old keys didn't work in the lock; my wife evidently had changed them while I was in jail. I remembered the back window where I gained entrance the month prior. I went to the back of the house and tried the window again. It was still broken so I climbed through again.

The hair on the back of my neck stood up and my stomach started to feel queasy. Abandonment, self-pity, and sorrow engulf me as I gazed at the empty living and dining rooms. I walked across the rooms, my footsteps echoing with each step. I went upstairs and looked into our bedroom closet. A few of the shirts and pants I wore to work were still there. I didn't need them but wanted to take everything, so I carried them downstairs and placed them in a pile in the middle of the living room. I walked through the kitchen next, and down the basement steps where my wife and I had argued and pushed one another. I saw the washer and dryer and the upright freezer.

I went into the rec room where I'd spent most of my time with the door closed getting high. I immediately wanted to use! My eyes scanned the room: a filing cabinet, a daybed with a small table in front of it where I used to chop up dope. Across from me was the stereo console with the color TV resting on top. I remembered sitting there many days and nights smoking and drinking with the television on for background noise. I started to sweat and my stomach was in knots. I couldn't think about anything other than using. I began to look on the rug for any little crumbs of crack, a practice I performed every time the dope was gone. There were many, many times I was on the floor feeling for bits of dope. I got down on my hands and knees, licked my finger and placed it on any tiny white speck I could find, then put it in my mouth to see if it was dope. I was fiending! It was automatic behavior.

While on my knees I realized that if I did find some dope and ingested it, I'd be off and running, and I wouldn't go back to Orca House. I jumped up, ran upstairs through the kitchen, and left through the front door. I was terrified. *What if I ingested a piece of dope when I was licking the floor?* My tongue started to feel numb; I was almost positive that I may have found a crumb.

I walked from Meadowbrook Road in Cleveland Heights to Orca House on East 89th and Chester. I'd never walked so fast in my life! I recited the Serenity Prayer over and over with every step I took. I was scared that I had fucked up. I knew that the first thing they would do when I got back to Orca would be to piss test me. *Oh shit! What did I do?! If I come out positive they'll kick me out and I can't go back to my mother's house and I don't want to sleep in my car again. I know I'll pick up again. I really want to be clean and sober and I screwed it up!* I walked faster and faster toward Orca, thinking the entire time about what I was going to do if I came up dirty. *I screwed up my life again. Why do I keep doing this shit?! I'm fucking worthless! I just ruined any chance I had to get clean!*

CHAPTER FOURTEEN

The Move

I ARRIVED at Orca just as dinner was starting. Fear, anxiety and sweat greeted Tyrone the monitor when I entered the front door.

"You gotta drop some urine for me," he said. I told him that I thought I might have used. Tyrone replied sternly, "What do you mean you think you used?! Either you did or you didn't!"

"It was like I had never left the basement... just picked up where I'd left off. I don't want to use but it was like I didn't have any defense against it. Before I knew it, I was on the basement floor searching for crumbs of dope," I said.

I was in a panic. I did not want to be kicked out of the house for a dirty urine. Tyrone told me that without the 12 steps in my life, I would continue to suffer from untreated alcoholism and drug addiction.

"If you don't work the steps then you're just wasting good 'get high' time. If nothing changes, nothing changes!"

Tyrone began to fill out the paperwork for the urinalysis. He gave me a small plastic cup with cap and escorted me to the bathroom. I said a prayer as I peed: *Oh God, please let this be clean!* I handed the container of urine to Tyrone, who had put on latex gloves. He placed a strip around the cup to test for temperature, making sure that I hadn't saved or used someone else's pee for the test. I signed a label and he signed below verifying it was my sample. It was then placed into an envelope and sealed. I initialed the envelope, and it was put in a secure box for the testing agency to pick it up. It would take a day to get the results.

Tyrone said I should eat because we were going to a 7:30 meeting. I was more nervous than hungry but I tried to eat something. On the way to the meeting I told my friend, Tyrone S., what had happened. Tyrone S. told me that I probably should have had someone go with me. This was one of the things that we were taught in treatment but I hadn't seen the need for until now. If we ever felt shaky about our sobriety or were going somewhere where there might be alcohol, we should take another sober person with us. I could see how this would have been useful in my situation. I really had to be vigilant when it came to sobriety.

Before going to bed for the evening, I got down on my knees and said the longest prayer I had ever said, asking a Higher Power to help me stay clean and sober. I especially prayed for the urine test to come back negative! I asked over and over again until my knees started to hurt. I didn't sleep very well, if at all, that night.

I started the day again on my knees, asking "God" to keep me clean and sober and that the urinalysis would come back negative. An entire day passed without mention of the results. I still had to get my stuff out of the house, but I didn't want to leave Orca, let alone enter that house again! I talked to my mother over the phone and she agreed to pay for a storage facility and for a small U-Haul to cart the stuff over there. That was a load off my mind. *If I could only levitate the crap out of the house and into the U-Haul!*

After dinner we went to a meeting. I started to enjoy the meetings, especially being able to share what was going on in my life with other people, something I NEVER would have considered doing previously. Before Orca, I'd sit down with a twelve pack and some dope and tell myself that a little buzz would help me solve whatever the problem was. Well, it did. Once I drank and smoked enough the problem vanished for the time being. The only drawback was that the problem was still there when I'd come down. Then I'd have to drink and use again to give me "insight" into the solution. The problem went away again, only to return once I came down. Drugs and alcohol were not the problem; they were the solution to my problems, at least temporarily.

My mother and wife told me that all I had to do was stop using dope and drink with moderation and I would be alright. I'd try to stop drinking and using and maybe I'd last a couple of days until I'd start feeling worse. *How am I supposed to deal with all the bullshit in my life without taking the edge off? Instead, you take away my solution to dealing with life and expect me to handle it gracefully without a sufficient substitute? Well, spare me that shit 'cause it don't work!* I'd tried countless times. Getting high was a primary function, like breathing. I couldn't start my day without getting high. I couldn't leave the house without being high. I couldn't go to a movie without being high. A good buzz would make everything more enjoyable, and the band lifestyle encouraged that. I felt privileged to be able to get high daily. *That's what a musician does, right?* I pitied the folks that had to wait for the weekends to get loaded. Every day was a weekend for me.

I asked my mother to drop off a book that I was given at the Cleveland Clinic while I was in detox at the psych ward: the Basic Text of *Narcotics Anonymous.* Most of the time after meetings, I didn't want to hang with the rest of the cats in the house watching TV or playing cards; it seemed like a waste of time. I started going upstairs more often to the weight room to workout and talk to my friend Tyrone, or read the daily recovery material that was given to us. If I actually *read* some of the Basic Text, I might get some information about how to stay clean.

My brain was foggy but not as bad as when I first arrived. At that time, I couldn't get through a sentence or comprehend what was read or said to me. My attention span was less than a few seconds and I was easily distracted. I pushed myself to focus on what I was reading and hearing, but I still had to reread sentences to get the meaning. I had an incentive to discipline myself: I wanted to stay clean and sober. I would hear recovered men and women say that they'd learned the solution to not picking up: the steps. I heard that there was a difference between white knuckled sobriety and allowing a power greater than myself remove the obsession to use. That was what I wanted. I knew that I *couldn't use* but wanted to be able to get to the point where I *didn't want* to use. Tyrone the monitor said: "The 12 steps are not for people who need it, they're for people who want it." I wanted it and was ready to go to any length to get and keep it!

My mother arranged to have my mail forwarded to Orca House. Overdue gas and electric bills started to arrive, along with statements and threats from MBNA and reminders from the two or three pawn shops on Euclid Avenue that were preparing to sell the items in their possession. Among those items was my 1978 Les Paul Custom guitar, an acoustic 12 string, and a silver brush and mirror set I had sneaked out of my mother's house. I had already lost one guitar by not being able to pay to get it out. Pawning or selling worked well when I needed to get dope, and when I ran out of my stuff I pawned my mother's. Once, I rummaged through her closet when she wasn't home and found a gold wedding band which I promptly sold and it was melted down. This was my mother's ring from her marriage to Percy that I didn't know about. Her only material remembrance of this man was from the ring that I had stolen, gone forever. One of many things I wasn't proud of. My conscience was working on me now that there was nothing to keep it at bay. Guilt from decisions to steal from the only real family I had overwhelmed me. *How do I get her silver brush set out of hock without her knowing I'd stolen it with no money?* I had to tell her.

I called my mom from the payphone and confessed. It confirmed what she had been thinking all along: her son was a thieving addict. I told her where the pawn ticket was and she bought back her own belongings. I was ashamed. She said that I had to figure out how to get my guitars out.

Another day passed and I asked about the results of the urinalysis.

"I'll let you know," Jennie said. "Just keep learning about recovery while you have a chance to!" And I did just that. But there was still the problem of getting my stuff out of the house before it was discarded. I asked Jennie if I could go back to my old house again to move my things into storage. "This time I'm making sure someone goes with you." Jennie knew that Tyrone S. and I had become friends. Ty had been in the house longer, and had escorted guys on brief trips to the clinic, so she asked him to go with me to help move my things, but mainly for support.

My mother picked us up the next day for the move. The entire way to U-Haul she complimented Tyrone on his sobriety and told him how much she appreciated his help. Tyrone told her a little about his family and about his mother passing before she had a chance to see him get sober.

"Well, you can be my son for now if you like," Mom said. Tyrone looked at me.

"So you mean this guy's my brother?" he asked.

"Yes, if that's alright." He was silent for a second or two.

"I can go for that," he said and laughed.

Tyrone and I rented the truck then went over to the house. I went through the back window and opened the front door for him. I was feeling more confident about being there with Tyrone present. He made a couple of jokes about me doing a B and E on my own house. I told him he was my accomplice and he shut up. I showed him around the house. We moved the clothes that I had left in the middle of the floor on my first trip, then went down the basement. I bragged about getting high down there. I pointed out the freezer, bed and TV that needed to be moved. He asked about the huge stereo console. I told him we could leave it.

"Good!" he said. I looked inside the stereo, and showed him 45s I had listened to while getting high. I dug deeper on the closed side of the record bin when my hand hit something. An anxious feeling swept over me. It was the cookie tin I used to hold my paraphernalia: broken glass stems, screens, pushers, razor blades and dope. I stashed it away so well that I couldn't find it before. I started to open it but Ty yanked it from my hands.

"Don't you want to see what's in there?" I asked.

"I already know what's in there and we don't need to see it, we need to get rid of it! If we don't get it away from us and out of this house then that's all we'll be thinking about," he said.

I agreed. We took the tin across the street and Ty tossed it into a dumpster behind an apartment building. We returned to the house to begin moving. It was a sight: two skinny crackheads trying to move a freezer from the basement into the truck. Even though I knew it was legal, it sure felt illegal and looked like it too from the street.

We managed to get the TV and daybed loaded and went to a storage facility. I paid for the locker with money my mother had given me and we moved everything into storage. That was the most physical labor that Tyrone and I had done in a long, long time! We were beat by the time we dropped off the truck and made it back to Orca. As soon as we walked through the door, we were piss tested. After, we ate dinner and went to a meeting with the rest of the guys. At lights out that night I got on my knees again and thanked "God" for putting Ty between me and a possible tragedy and was thankful that everything happened the way it did. I was even thankful for my backache!

The next day our urinalyses came back from the previous day: both clean. Nothing was ever said about the test results from my previous urine test. I never asked again.

CHAPTER FIFTEEN

Journey in Recovery

I REALIZED at this point that I was powerless over drugs and alcohol. No matter how much I didn't want to use I found myself absorbed in thoughts of using without adequate defense. The thing that saved me outside of Orca was when I had another person with me to intervene whenever I tried to pick up. It was not possible have someone at my side 24 hours a day, nor could I live secluded in treatment for the rest of my life. It made sense to apply the same solution in my life that had helped Tyrone the monitor, my sponsor, and numerous men and women I had met and heard speak at meetings. Tyrone E. would say: "Even if you don't work the steps the steps still work, they just won't be working for YOU!"

I called my sponsor from the payphone.

"I want to get busy on the steps!" He said he would pick me up and take me to his homegroup if it was alright with my counselor. I told Jennie what my sponsor said and she allowed me to go with him. The name of my sponsor's homegroup was Listen To Learn. I immediately made it my homegroup as well. Only one other person in the house had a sponsor at that time and he would soon be "coined out" (receiving a sobriety coin and completion certificate) from the house and then on to IOP (Intensive Out Patient) after that for six weeks. My sponsor said he would guide me through the first three steps and start on the fourth after our homegroup meeting. I was ready to do this thing! I kept hearing how my life would change by working the steps and I couldn't wait to have at it.

The meeting was held at the Langston Hughes building on East 89th, and was close to being condemned. Plaster was falling off the walls and ceiling, dust and dirt everywhere, and a toilet that you had to pour water into in order to flush. Only about three people showed for my first meeting there. I didn't care what the place looked like or how many people showed up; I just wanted to start working the steps that everyone talked about. When the meeting was over my sponsor took out the third edition of the book *Alcoholics Anonymous* and gave me a copy. We said the Serenity Prayer and I turned to the title page: "Alcoholics Anonymous, the story of How Many Thousands of Men and Women Have Recovered from Alcoholism, Third Edition."

My sponsor assured me that the 12 steps worked on crackheads and dope fiends too. If I had trouble with the word alcohol, I could plug in heroin or crack. At this time I still thought my main problems were crack and heroin but not alcohol as much. I had forgotten about the four or five DUIs and the jail time I served in Portage County for hitting a tree while drunk. He asked me to read aloud, and he would do his best to answer any questions I had. Anything that he couldn't answer he would ask his sponsor or get the answer for me from someone else in recovery. We turned to the Preface of the third edition. It said that the first 164 pages of the book was the program of recovery and has remained untouched throughout revisions to the second and third editions. My sponsor asked what that meant to me. I told him I hadn't a clue.

"If something ain't broke, don't fix it," he said. It has worked for millions of alcoholics since the first edition in 1939. He also stated that the Doctor's Opinion was also unaltered. We moved on to the Foreword of the first edition as it appeared in in 1939:

> We, of Alcoholics Anonymous, are more than one hundred men and women who have recovered from a seemingly hopeless state of mind and body. To show other alcoholics precisely how we have recovered is the main purpose of this book.

"Does this mean that if I read this book I'll learn how to recover?"

"If you apply what you read in the first 164 pages of this book to your life you will recover from a seemingly hopeless state of mind and body. That, my friend, is a guarantee," he said.

My journey in recovery had begun. My sponsor and I read aloud as he took me through my first three steps. We got on our knees and I repeated the third step prayer: "God, I offer myself to thee to build with me and to do with me as thou wilt. Relieve me from the bondage of self, that I may better do thy will. Take away my difficulties that victory over them may bear witness to those that I would help of thy power, thy love and thy way of life. May I do thy will always." For the first time in years I actually felt as though I was part of something bigger than myself. It was a relief to stop fighting and trying to figure everything out. *I allow and don't resist, for a change...I surrender.* I took my sponsor's advice to "trust the process." I felt as though a weight had been lifted, but he told me that we weren't done yet. I was walking on clouds, though, and was sure that this prayer alone would do the trick. He talked about a fourth step inventory: "We have to get down to causes and conditions."

It was time to take a look at me; the one thing I had avoided for years. I knew that if I took an honest look at myself that I wouldn't like what I saw. I had spent years covering up, rationalizing and justifying my actions. I was sure that most of my problems and resentments were a result of someone or something, but never me. Hell, the last thing I wanted to do when I got high was look at me!

My sponsor gave me an inventory packet that contained: Resentments, Fears, People I've Harmed, and Sexual Conduct (or as I like to say, sexual misconduct). I was happy to see the Resentment list because I had a million of them! I started to sweat when I thought about having to list Fears and Sexual Conduct. As far as harming people? I was sure that I was going to break down and need to be sedated when writing about that. After all, I got very high so I wouldn't have to think about all the dirt I'd done and the people I'd harmed along the way.

My sponsor could smell the smoke coming out of my ears.

"Just concentrate on resentments first."

"No problem, I'll be glad to!" The Resentment list consisted of three columns from left to right:

1) I'm resentful at:
2) The cause:
3) It affects my:

My sponsor instructed me to write down ALL of my resentments in the first column. I told him I would need more than a page and he suggested that I make plenty of copies before I start.

"List the cause of each resentment only after you've listed all you can think of," he said. "Examples of resentments could be people, institutions, courts, taxes, child support, your wife."

I couldn't wait to start!

As I walked through the side door of Orca that night I felt that I had been introduced to something entirely new and foreign. I was on the verge of doing a new thing that could possibly change my life. It was all so different. I had never before asked any man to help me stay sober. The last thing I had read of any importance before that evening was *Charlie and The Chocolate Factory* in sixth grade! And I had never, ever gotten on my knees, held hands with another man and recited a prayer!

I found my good friend Tyrone S. and blurted out everything that happened that evening.

"That's why I don't need a sponsor...I don't want some dude telling me what to do....I'm a grown ass man," Tyrone said. I told him that our *very best* thinking had gotten us seats at Orca House; perhaps we should learn how to stay clean and sober from somebody else.

In May, 2001, I celebrated my 46th birthday on the 28th with a four hour pass. My mother took me to her house where she made dinner, gave me a birthday card, and drove me back to Orca with a lemon cake she made with specific instructions to share it with Tyrone S. and the rest of the guys in the house. Everyone was happy to see the cake. I expected a consolidated Happy Birthday from my peers but got instead: "Tell your mom thanks for the cake." Here was another resentment to add to my list!

Guys were coming and going from the house. Some completed their stay while others just left; some through the front door and one from the second floor fire escape. The one on the second floor had been using the fire escape to leave the house nightly to drink. He would always turn in for bed early and we wouldn't see him until the next morning. One evening he left the bedroom window open and the wind had blown his door ajar. Tyrone the monitor entered his room to find that not only was he missing, he also had a 12-pack of empty Budweiser cans in his closet. Tyrone locked the bedroom window and waited for the guy to come back, knowing he would have to use the front door. We heard the doorbell ring. Tyrone E. met the guy at the front door with: "Pack up yo shit and go!" Tyrone also made him take the empty beer cans with him.

A NEW BATCH of guys were in the house. The only original left from when I entered in April was my friend, Tyrone S., and we became peer leaders. Leading by example and monitoring everyone was our job. We were like the house police. I told Tyrone E. that I didn't like being a snitch and my peers didn't dig it too much either.

"Learn to stand up for your sobriety," Tyrone said. "If you don't stand for something, you'll fall for anything." If someone threatened our sobriety then we had an obligation to report it. Similarly, if someone was doing something they shouldn't be doing, it could affect the entire house. "Your actions can't be based on whether or not someone will like you. Learn to follow principles and lead by authority and example." Two things that the people-pleaser in me hated to do. Most of the guys in the house believed that "snitches get stitches!" I talked to my sponsor about it, and he believed that Ty and I were made peer leaders because we had shown growth.

I finished the resentment part of my 4th step inventory. I'd been working on it every night after our nightly meetings before lights out. My sponsor told me to move on to the "People I've Harmed" section. I list every member of my immediate family with my mother at the top. My sponsor told me to add my name as well. I became sad thinking about what my actions had done to my children. Self-pity with low self-esteem covered me like a blanket. I couldn't medicate this feeling away; could only learn how to go through it. One tool I was given to abate the feelings of worthlessness was the therapeutic value of talking to another addict. I was sharing everything with my friend, Tyrone S., and I found that I no longer had to hang onto painful feelings. This was something I couldn't do while out getting high with other people. Nobody wanted to hear about how I felt or who I'd hurt. They'd say: "Save that shit and pass the pipe!" And I'd cover up my feelings with more smoke. I was going to be able to dump even more on to my sponsor when it was time for my fifth step. Doing things differently brought about different results. I was used to doing the same thing over and over again and expecting different results: the definition of insanity!

CHAPTER SIXTEEN

Founders Day

JUNE ARRIVED bringing with it talk about a carwash to raise money to go to Founders Day.

"Who's washing cars?" I asked.

"You're washing cars!"

I didn't remember the last time I'd washed my car or changed the oil. As long as I could see through the windshield I was cool. I did use Windex on the inside of the windshield occasionally when it started turning sticky and brown from nicotine. It was time to put oil in when I heard the engine knocking.

What is this Founders Day crap?

Founders Day is the celebration of the birth of Alcoholics Anonymous, and it takes place annually in Akron, Ohio around the first or second weekend in June. Our house, and the women's house, had to raise money to go. The house monitors said we'd never forget the experience as recovered folks from all over the world attend. Tyrone E. said there was nothing like holding hands with a few thousand people and saying the Lord's Prayer in unison. I was interested in the trip but not thrilled about washing cars.

We made flyers to advertise the carwash, which was the following weekend. Many Orca alums brought their cars, and my mother even showed up with her car. I would never forget my mom's smile as she watched her 46-year-old son wash her car. For the first time in years I felt as though I was of service to someone other than myself. I was able to label this feeling: gratitude. Everyone was enthusiastic about the carwash, and some cats held signs on the street corner, yelling at people driving by to pull in. One guy screamed: "If you don't let us wash your car I'm going to start drinking again!" He was replaced and told that the world couldn't care less if he had a drink or not, but, *he should care!*

At 5 p.m., we wound things down so that we could eat and go to a meeting. I continued to have a feeling of contentment and satisfaction throughout the rest of the evening. I got on my knees and thanked a God I had never really believed in for a good day. I couldn't remember the last time that I had an entire day void of turmoil. I slept well that night.

The next morning my back, legs, arms, feet and even my toes screamed in pain. I got on my knees and asked God to keep me sober for the day. We had another day ahead washing cars. What was a blessing on Saturday felt like unpaid labor on Sunday! Everyone was moving slow, and someone said that I was out of shape. *No shit!* House chores still had to be done before we washed cars. I mopped the upstairs bathroom and cleaned the toilets, complaining with every stroke. A monitor named Chris said: "Where's your gratitude this morning?"

"It must still be in my bed!"

I started thinking about my mother's encouraging smile from the day before and stopped grumbling for awhile. Everyone seemed to enjoy the camaraderie again as we washed more cars. The action of doing something for someone else enabled us to take our minds off of our favorite subject: ourselves. We got *out of self.* By the end of the day my gratitude had returned. We collectively made enough money to rent two buses to transport us to Founders Day. Everyone in the house felt a little closer to one another.

The week of Founders Day, the women's house cooked ribs and potato salad for the trip. Two white buses pulled into the parking lot and we carried food and soft drinks to the baggage area. This was the first time that clients from the Orca men's and women's houses went anywhere together. Women and men were housed separately in order to keep the focus on sobriety. Women were allowed to come to the men's house for one meeting a week. They had to sit in front at the meeting and not have any contact with us. Many of us fell in lust every time we saw them and had made plans to get with them on the trip when no one was supervising. Tyrone E. told us to keep the focus on ourselves: "The only thing two sick people can do together is to get sicker! Leave them girls alone!"

The bus was laid out! It was similar to an airplane in that it had individual controls to adjust personal air flow and color TV monitors every third row on both sides. We had been on several outings before but nothing like this. At one point during my stay at Orca, we went to Karamu to see a play. I was excited and told Tyrone S. that my dad started his acting career there, and I couldn't wait to find pictures of him on the walls. After we saw the play, Tyrone S. and I wandered around the building looking for a photo collection, but there wasn't any mention of my father or any pictures. I was embarrassed and my self-esteem took a dive. It was then that I promised myself not to make my self-worth dependent upon another, something I had done my entire life. I had to start being okay with me just the way I was at that or any moment. I would be given more opportunities to practice my new conviction.

We also had an opportunity to go see the all-female basketball team, the Cleveland Rockers. We didn't care if they won or lost, just wanted to see women running around jumping up and down! Although very crude in our thoughts, the idea that we could enjoy activities without being drunk or high was a welcome revelation.

The trip to Akron was full of anticipation. We watched a shoot 'em up video on TV screens and tried to mess with the women at the front of the bus. After being reprimanded a few times we decided to just check out the video. When we arrived, the monitors did a head count, then we transported the food and pop to the student union of Akron University where the event is held annually. We received name tags and information regarding the events. To our surprise, we were permitted to go off to the events on our own, with the women, for three hours! The only problem was that Tyrone S. and I were peer leaders and we were responsible for our guys. The women had a couple of peer leaders too. Ty and I were charged with keeping 14 horny dudes (16 if you counted us) out of the bushes! There were meetings, panel groups and plays going on through-out the day. I made a deal with Tyrone that I'd take a couple of guys to a one of the meetings and then come back and switch with him. He agreed and stayed with a few guys and women until I came back. There was a 2 p.m. meeting in the arena, and I felt like I was part of something big. People came up to me and said: "Hi, Dave, welcome home." I couldn't figure out how they knew my name for the longest time, until I remembered the tag on my chest.

After the meeting we walked back to where Tyrone and the rest of the guys were. These cats hadn't moved and neither had the women! They were all caught up in the activities. Ty looked very comfortable, as well. He told me to go ahead if I wanted to, so I left with another guy on a short bus trip to the house of a founding member of A.A., Dr. Bob. On the porch of the house, a guy said, "welcome home" and I continued to feel as though I belonged.

Some time after leaving Orca permanently, I would see the guy that I went with to Dr. Bob's house, standing in front of the women's shelter panhandling. He asked me if I was still sober and I said yes. He said: "I knew you'd still be," and asked me for some money. I haven't seen him since.

I FELT A spiritual high at Founders Day and vowed to return every year. I began to look at life differently. No longer did I see the dog eat dog, eye for an eye, my life sucks world. I began to see events in my life as learning experiences. I knew a power was working in my life to guide me. Even those experiences and situations that I would have thought painful ear-lier, I could see as beneficial. I once thought that being in active addic-tion and losing my family was the worst thing that ever happened to me. But, had that not occurred, I may never have learned how to live life in a different way. All of the material things and trappings of a supposedly successful lifestyle nearly killed me. That superficial crap made me feel as though I was okay. When I lost the house, the wife, the job, the car and the kids I felt worthless. My image of being okay in the world was shattered. Only by losing everything, my soul included, was I able to surrender and humble myself to ask for help. My ego had to be deflated. When I finally stopped fighting and started listening, my life started to change. As Tyrone E. would say: "Surrender to win."

My PARENTS Clayton Smeltz (later Corbin) and Inez Hall Smeltz. *At left:* A headshot of Clayton.

Below: A ticket from "The Negro as Playwright" a drama reading session in New York City, 1954.

Opposite page, top: My grandparents Inez Anderson Hall, and Dr. William Hall.

```
         Special Drama Reading Session.

          "THE NEGRO AS PLAYWRIGHT"

     Featuring scripts by Langston Hughes,
     Countee Cullen, Louis Peterson, Owen
     Dodson, Richard Wright and Herbert
     Greggs.
               ACTORS PARTICIPATING
     Virginia Anton, Charles Bettis, Clayton Smeltz
             of Karamu Theatre, Cleveland, Ohio
               Staged by  RAOUL ABDUL

     THURSDAY, MAY 27th, 1954              8:15 P.M.
     Countee Cullen Br. Library      104 West 136 St.

               Admission Free
```

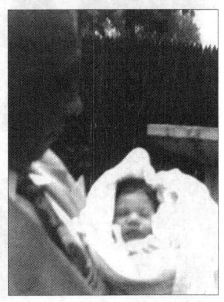

WITH Santa Claus when I was approximately five years old, and with my grandfather, June, 1955.

MUGSHOTS. The one on the right was passed around at Cleveland Heights jail for the officers' amusement.

IN MY BUNK at The Salvation Army's P.A.S.S. program, January 2002.

A PRIVATE DINNER with Mom, August, 2007.

My Best Friend and brother in recovery Tyrone Saunders with Clean House, Inc. materials at an event.

Clean House purchased this building at 11910 Buckeye Road in Cleveland, Ohio November, 2013. We are hard at work rehabilitating this vandalized property.

PERFORMING with I-Tal at the Grog Shop in Cleveland Heights in 2012.

I-TAL *(top, from left):* George Gordon, me, Chris Dunmore, John Wagner, Carlos Jones, Russ Richards, and Bob Caruso. *Above:* Band co-founder Dave Valentine.

At right: Teaching moves to Dean Dietrich, Jr. at a Clean House, Inc. Meditation and Mindfulness fundraiser, April, 2014.

Jennifer Colley

CHAPTER SEVENTEEN

104 Days

I HAD BEEN at Orca for nearly three months. I was in phase three which meant that I had been there long enough to fulfill my plan of care, and was able to leave the facility during the day unescorted. The first place I walked to was the library. I had become a voracious reader of anything having to do with recovery and spirituality. I signed up for a library card and checked out *The Bhagavad Gita* and a book written by A.A. cofounder, Bill Wilson, *The Twelve Steps and Twelve Traditions of Alcoholics Anonymous*. I read all day sitting near a church that had a small park next to it.

For the first time in a very long while I actually enjoyed the sound of birds chirping. In my active addiction days, the sound of chirping birds meant that I'd been up all night. I noticed things that I had previously taken for granted, like watching squirrels chase one another up and down trees. I felt the hair on my arms wiggle as the spring breeze caressed me. The grass even seemed to be greener in color! Although my only source of income was five dollars per week from my mother, I was wealthy in other areas of my life: I was clean and sober for that day and it meant more to me than anything. It meant that I had a chance at life as long as I didn't pick up. It meant that all things were possible. It meant that I had been granted the opportunity to live a new life.

I'd return to Orca by 5 p.m. for dinner and then go to a nightly meeting with my peers. Mail continued to arrive for me at the house. The wreckage of my past continued to haunt my present. I received bank statements for insufficient funds; notifications from the pawn shop informing me that my guitars and other stuff I stole from my mother would be put out for sale; and letters from my probation officer stating that if I missed any additional appointments, a warrant would be issued for my arrest. I had forgotten that I was on probation for domestic violence! Not to mention that MBNA wanted their seven thousand dollars, and my estranged wife had filed for divorce.

My heart sank. Feelings of worthlessness and self-pity began to creep in. Rather than wallow in the pain of the problem, I began to do something different: I used the tools I'd been given to work on the solution. I talked to another addict. The Basic Text of *Narcotics Anonymous* states that the therapeutic value of one addict sharing with another is without parallel. I opened up and shared with anyone who would listen. As Tyrone E. would say: "A problem shared is a problem cut in half."

My sponsor had taken me through the steps and it was time to live them. He made sure that I had a thorough understanding, and continued to take me to his homegroup meeting every Monday. Then, one day it dawned on me that it had been a while since I had thought about picking up a drink or a drug. I actually started to feel better physically. I knew that my time at the house was coming to an end. Guys were coming and going. Tyrone S. and I were the only two guys still there from our original group 90 days prior. I also figured it was time to go when the monitors and counselors began to ask: "What are your plans when you leave?" Tyrone S. was waiting to be approved for section 8 housing. He couldn't go back to live in the same environment he had left. Neither could I.

I had a one on one with Tyrone E. about leaving, as I didn't have anywhere to go. I couldn't go back to my mother's house; she had hinted that she preferred less drama. Plus, I had plenty of memories using in that environment. I needed more discipline and a solid foundation in recovery to build upon, as I was scared that I might use again. Tyrone E. suggested I go to further treatment. He told me about a transitional sober housing program run by the Salvation Army, called PASS (**P**ick Up, **A**ssessment, **S**helter and **S**ervices). Meetings, group discussions, and Life Skill classes to teach money management were offered. Plus, they had free legal advice and representation which I would soon require. Savings accounts were opened for clients at the facility, and clients received free food and housing in a sober atmosphere. It sounded perfect! I told my counselor that I wanted to go to further treatment in the PASS program. She said she would try to get a bed for me, and set up my "out" date; I'd be leaving Orca in two weeks!

"What if there isn't a bed for me at the Salvation Army?"

"There's always room at the homeless shelter at 2100 Lakeside until something opens up. Until then, I suggest you pray and trust the process." I was in a haze as I walked out of her office. My old friends, Worry and Anxiety, pounced upon me out of nowhere. I immediately called my sponsor from the house payphone.

"They're kicking me out in two weeks and I might have to stay at the men's shelter!" My sponsor told me to calm down, reminded me that I had been there before for an evening, and that I may not even have to go there.

"Besides," he said, "it's two weeks away! It's time for you to start using the steps that you have in your life now." He reminded me of a passage in the Big Book after the 10th step: "And we have ceased fighting anything or anyone including alcohol." I took that statement and ran with it. All my life I had manipulated, adjusted and skewed things to go my way. I always needed to know how things would work out in advance. That was always my safety net; I had to control the situation. I felt powerless in this situation. If I am powerless (which is the problem) then I had to find a power greater than me to solve it. When I admitted to being powerless over dope and alcohol in the first step of the 12 steps, I was taken to the second step which provided the solution: "Came to believe that a power greater than ourselves could restore us to sanity." The steps enabled me to find a power that relieved me of the obsession to drink. If it could do that then why couldn't it work on this problem?

I recited the Serenity Prayer just as I had when it was introduced to me my first day of treatment. I asked the God of my personal understanding to grant me the grace to do His will. I then put my faith in this power that everything would work out for the best. I also knew that sometime His version of what is best for me clashed with my expectations! I had to practice acceptance of whatever the outcome but for now I could only do what was in front of me. Once again, Tyrone E. said it best: "If you're going to pray, why worry? And, if you're going to worry, why pray?" So I prayed.

My last two weeks at the house were a trip. Until then, I had been sheltered from the consequences of my actions while in active addiction. It was time to face things that I had neatly tucked away and hoped would disappear. All of these things coming at me at once brought on the feelings of worry, anxiety, low self-esteem: the same crap I felt when getting high. Since getting high was no longer an option, I had to use the tools I'd been given at Orca. The first thing I did was to tell people what was going on in my life and not try to solve it all with my thinking; the same thinking that got me to Orca House. You can't solve a problem with the same mind that created it! I needed outside input. This was most definitely a different course of action for me. I shared with my friend, Tyrone S.

"What did your sponsor say?"

I shared with Tyrone E. the monitor.

"What did your sponsor say?"

I shared with the rest of my peers at a group discussion and they too wanted to know what my sponsor said. I thought, *Maybe I should call my sponsor?*

My sponsor always had a way of slowing me down. Allowing others to have input in my life became the component for change in my actions. When I complained about what others had done to me he asked: "What part did you play in it?" I didn't want to hear that! I was more comfortable blaming others and, once again, not taking responsibility for my behavior. He reminded me of three sayings I'd seen on placards at the majority of meetings we'd attended:

First Things First

Easy Does It

Keep It Simple

I previously regarded these signs as wall filler, to cover cracks perhaps.

As my sponsor explained them one at a time, I began to see how I could apply these to my immediate situation.

Things that required my attention: 1) file for bankruptcy 2) get items I took from my mother out of the pawn shop before they were sold 3) schedule a meeting with probation officer to avoid a warrant being issued for my arrest, and, 4) respond to the divorce filing.

First Things First: I chose the task that required immediate attention, then second most urgent, and so on, in descending order of importance. I would first contact my mother and tell her that we needed to get some of her things out of pawn. To add insult to her injury, she would have to pay to get her stuff back! This was not an easy phone call to make. Second, I made sure I had a bus pass and knew the schedule so I could make an appearance for my probation officer. Third, I would find an attorney to represent me for my impending divorce, and fourth, file for bankruptcy.

Easy Does It: I did one thing at a time, in order; I didn't skip from one to three and then back to two. In the past, I always tried to do everything at once and it would frustrate me so much that I would wind up doing nothing at all.

Keep It Simple: I didn't put any more thought into it than was required. Sometimes I could make something much more problematic by going over and over it again searching for answers and outcomes. I learned to take the action and leave the results in God's hands. I was reminded that God had not brought me this far to just drop me. Without realizing it, I had become responsible.

Two days before I was scheduled to leave treatment my counselor said that there was a bed waiting for me at the Salvation Army PASS program. That night before lights out, I stayed on my knees and thanked the God that I began to see working in my life. I hardly slept that night. As soon as I arose the next morning, I got on my knees once again. My prayers were very simple: "God, thank you for allowing me to wake up sober. Please continue to keep me clean and sober today."

This was my last day at Orca House. I had been there 104 days.

CHAPTER EIGHTEEN

Don't Let Fluker Knock You Off Your Square

WHEN A CLIENT is scheduled to leave Orca House, he has to write down what he plans to do when he goes: his immediate plans and an ongoing plan for recovery. Counselors, staff and peers evaluate the plan and suggest what he may have overlooked. I had participated in one client's outgoing plans and now it was my turn. A staff member named Clarence Fluker was feared by all those leaving. He pissed off a lot of guys by finding holes in their plan of recovery. Tyrone S. told me before I wrote out my plan: "Don't let Fluker knock you off your square." I witnessed guys throw chairs and swear at Fluker, and he'd respond by saying: "If I'm pissing you off in here, what are you going to do when your boss or your woman pisses you off? You're gonna get high!" Guys got bent out of shape and screamed things like: "You don't know me! You don't know what I'll do!" And Fluker would reply: "You're gonna pick up!"

I was sure he wouldn't upset me because I had the best plan of action of anyone; he wouldn't find any loopholes in my blueprint for recovery! There were three headings we were to write under:

1) What I Have
2) What I Need
3) What I'm Going To Do

Under "What I Have" I wrote: God, the 12 steps, a sponsor, a big book, a Basic Text, a homegroup and a support system. Under "What I Need": A job, sobriety, a place to live and food to eat. "What I'm Going to Do": I'm going to live in transitional housing within a sober environment, I'm going to a meeting and I'll also attend aftercare at Orca two times a week for six weeks. I patted myself on the back over the perfection of my plan and asked Tyrone S. if he'd seen a better one. He said it looked good to him, so that was all the confirmation I needed. After lunch, I found myself in the Hot Seat. I stood next to the blackboard and prepared to dazzle everyone with the best plan of recovery they'd ever seen. I started to read what I had written on the board, when I was interrupted.

"You have everything except fear; aren't you scared?" Fluker asked me. I told him no. "You should be! You'd better respect and fear your enemy. You're fresh out of treatment; safe inside these walls. What are you going to do when you get out there?! That's where the *real* recovery begins; this is just discovery in here. What are you gonna do out there? I know, you'll do what you always did, YOU'LL GET HIGH!" I felt the hair on the back of my neck begin to stand up and my stomach got tight. It took everything in me not to tell him to FUCK OFF! I glanced over at Tyrone S. and he was shaking his head slowly from side to side as if to say, *Don't do it, Dave!*

I took a deep breath. "Honestly, I do have some fear."

"You'd better. Go on to the next one."

"I need a job, sobriety—"

"You need a solid foundation in recovery before you get a job or your first paycheck you'll GET HIGH!" My fists tightened, my teeth clenched and I began to shake. This time when I looked at Tyrone S., he had his head down, waiting for the inevitable. "WELL?" asked Fluker. I didn't say anything for a few seconds which felt like minutes. I didn't know it at the time but I was learning how to respond to a situation rather than react to it. Fluker was also teaching me humility, as I had to remain open minded to suggestions. I remembered what Tyrone E. would say: "You can't graft a new idea onto a closed mind."

No matter how much I wanted to disagree with him, I had to accept what he was saying, as he had been sober much longer than I. One thing was certain, it took everything I had to hold my tongue, not pout, fight back or run away; my usual response to confrontation. He asked me if I had anything else to say. To my amazement "thank you" came out of my mouth.

"You're welcome. Don't pick up and good luck."

The time had come to be coined out by my peers. We got into a circle and everyone said something about me and wished me luck. We were all scared to leave, just like Fluker said. We had all come from different backgrounds but had one thing in common: once we picked up a mood or mind altering substance we couldn't stop. When my peers wished me the best, they were also praying for their own sobriety. I was given a 24 hour a day coin. Tyrone E. said: "Hold onto this coin at all times and if someone offers you a drink, put this coin in your mouth and swallow it. And if you want to buy some dope, pay for it with this coin and see if you get any!" We put our arms around one another's shoulders and said the Lord's Prayer together. I went upstairs and got the two plastic garbage bags containing my belongings. I tried to hold back tears as I said good-bye and got in the house van to be driven to The Salvation Army. Orca House had saved my life.

A SIDE NOTE: Clarence Fluker died February, 2013 from cancer. The last time I saw him was at a mutual friend's funeral in August, 2012. He came up to me and gave me a hug. With a tear rolling down my cheek I looked him straight in his eyes and said: "You know, I stayed sober for my first year out of spite. You said I was going to get high and I wanted to prove you wrong." He smiled and said: "I'm glad you did." Thank you for helping me, Mr. Fluker. May you rest in peace.

CHAPTER NINETEEN

P.A.S.S.

THE VAN DRIVER took me to a single level brick building in downtown Cleveland. I got my belongings and walked up to the steel door. There was a video camera above the doorway and an intercom. I pushed the buzzer and a voice whined through the intercom, sounding like someone taking my order at a drive thru: "Can I help you?" I told the disembodied voice my name, that I was from Orca, and that I was supposed to have a bed there. The door buzzed and I went in. Painted over the entrance to the common area were the words: "Those who do not remember their past are liable to repeat it." Made sense to me!

I walked down the hall to an office on the right, where there was a room with security camera monitors. The guy that buzzed me in told me to sit down in the dining/common area. There were a few couches, chairs and long tables; it looked like an army mess hall except for the wide screen TV on the far wall. On my left was a long counter attached to the kitchen and next to the kitchen were three or four offices. To my immediate right I noticed doors on either side of a long hallway with guys ducking in and out of rooms. I could also hear toilets flushing and showers running.

A guy came out of an office and introduced himself as Ron Reinhardt. He had a long white beard and looked like Santa Claus, though I kept that to myself. He gave me a booklet of rules and regulations and told me: "Whatever you do, don't use 'cause it's grounds for immediate dismissal." Was cool with me; I wanted to be in a sober living environment. He took me on a little tour of the place, walking down a hall that ran parallel to the other long hallway. We passed a combination shower room and bathroom, and he said that I was one of about 72 men living there. *Oh great... I'm really not looking forward to showering, peeing and pooping around a bunch of dudes. At least Orca had separate shower stalls!* We continued down the hall past a few more brown doors and into another common area in the rear of the facility. At a large conference table were a bunch of guys having a 12 step meeting. Things were looking up until I heard: "You must be the new dude!" *I'm the friggin' new dude again!* With so many guys in that place my hope for a single room was out of the question. I just hoped that I would get along with 'em.

Reinhardt saw one of my new roommates at the table and told him to show me where I'd be bunking. *Crap! Sounds like bunk beds!* We walked back up the opposite hall and stopped at room number 11. Opening the door, it was dark as hell in there. My roommate said: "We keep the shades drawn to keep it cool in here." I saw a single bed in front of me, and to my far left and right I spied double bunk beds. I asked him if I could have the single. "Hell no! That's Eddie's bed! You're on the bottom bunk on the right in the corner over there." *Oh, this is just wonderful. I'm the fifth guy in a five man room!* All sorts of scenarios ran through my head. I asked about a door to my left. "Oh, that's the shower and toilet." *Yay, redemption. I'll just stay in the bathroom my entire time here.* Another guy bursts into the room. "Whose shit is this on my bed?!" *This must be Eddie!*

I took my bags off of Eddie's bed and placed them in the corner next to my bunk. Fortunately, I had the lower bunk. The guy in the lower bunk across from me had draped sheets around the outside of his bed for privacy. He also had a light, small TV, and cassette player with headphones and a bunch of recovery tapes. Pretty classy! I wanted my privacy too so I wrapped a sheet around my bed, reminding me of when, as a kid, I'd make a fort by hanging sheets over chairs and tables. Now I'm forty something and doing the same thing.

The bunk above the guy across the way was empty and sheetless. I asked him who stayed up there. "Oh, that's the relapse bed; the last three guys that slept up there relapsed and got booted out." Although I felt remorse for the last guy that slept up there, I was elated that there was one less dude in the room, at least for now. I was given sheets, a pillowcase and blanket, and told to use the bottom drawer of a five drawer cabinet for my belongings. I put my sheets on the bed and stretched the too small pillowcase over a funky looking pillow. I lay down on my bed, closed my eyes and wondered how my daughters were doing. *Do they miss me?* Tears welled up in my eyes. *So...this is my new home.* I thought about everything leading up to this point in my life. I was happy that I was not out on the street fiending for another hit. Everything that I believed to be part of my identity — children, wife, home, job, record collection, band — were gone. All that was left was me and God. I was starting a second life. A sober life. And, in order to be filled up, I first had to be emptied of everything. I had to trust in this God thing, otherwise, I knew I would feel hopeless again. I couldn't think of a better way to build a relationship with God when that was all I had. I had to have faith in something.

"CHOW TIME!" someone screamed. *Wow, just like treatment!* The dude across from me jumped out of bed and ran down the hall, and I figured I should follow him. It was my first dinner at the shelter. I stood in a single file line that wrapped around the dining room. No one could eat until everyone was served and seated. The monitor asked for two volunteers to wash dishes, pots and pans after dinner. When no one volunteered, which happened often, he chose two people. Someone was then selected to say grace and we'd eat.

My greatest fears were to wash all the filthy dishes and to be called on to say grace! After dinner I was assigned the chore of washing out the canteen (a truck with a small kitchen) every night when it returned to the shelter. It was loaded with hot food nightly and driven to areas around Cleveland to feed the hungry and homeless. The truck was a disaster whenever it returned: full of dried food and bread crumbs. I had to help a guy named Reno, and we'd get the detergent, buckets and mops every night around 10 p.m. when the canteen came back. We swept it out, wiped down the counters and then mopped the floor. I enjoyed getting to know Reno, and would tell him how I was feeling. He'd tolerate my little self-pity trips for a minute or two and then tell me: "Man up!" Reno was my first friend at the shelter.

I had a curfew for the first 30 days at PASS: 9 p.m. weekdays and 11 p.m. on weekends. My sponsor would come by to take me to our homegroup meeting on Mondays, and there was an in-house meeting at PASS on Thursdays. I went to Orca men's alumni meetings on Fridays, a meeting at Calvary Church on Saturdays, and on Sundays a meeting at the V.A. I got bus passes through the facility, and still frequented the library downtown. I always had a supply of reading material available. Most of the time I could be found in my bunk reading about recovery or spirituality.

There was always something going on at the shelter. Guys playing cards, watching TV, making food runs or just plain old talking shit to one another. I never really got into hanging out with the guys, as my interests were changing. My priority was to stay sober. I had been reminded by my sponsor that I didn't have to pay for anything, my room and board was free, so I might want to show my appreciation in some way. Also, by getting outside of myself and focusing on being of service I would not concentrate on missing my daughters so much. So, every once in awhile, I volunteered to wash dishes after dinner. I had to scrape off leftover food from plates that were piled up on the racks; rinse them with a small pressure hose; and place them in one of the two industrial strength dishwashers. After my first time completing this task I felt as though I had accomplished a great feat, as I had washed more than seventy dishes and sets of silverware.

As I prepared to leave the kitchen, the cook told me that I wasn't done. He pointed to all of the pots and pans used to prepare the meal; I had to wash those too! The pots and pans had to be soaked in hot water and scrubbed, with the largest Brillo pad I had ever seen, in order to remove the burned-on food. Meanwhile, the first dishwashing machine is emitting steam and heat so I was sweating like a slave trying to keep my balance on the slippery, water soaked tile floor. After the last pot was hand dried, I once again patted myself on the back for the swell job I had done. The cook returned and asked if I had finished. I told him I had and was going outside to smoke. He said: "No problem... Right after you mop the kitchen floor!" I mumbled back: "This shit never ends." To which he responded: "Where's your gratitude?" *Did he hear that shit from my sponsor?!*

I started meeting more guys in the complex. Some were about recovery, and others were about taking a break from the street. I talked with everyone but was more open with those who really wanted to stay clean. There was plenty of food and snacks to eat at night. I had been hitting up some sweet stuff when suddenly I felt tremendous pain in my mouth. I hadn't been to the dentist in some time. As a matter of fact, the last time was when I had a root canal done when I was working.

The pain got worse as the days passed and then one day as I was eating dinner I felt something hard with my tongue. I spit it out and discovered it was part of a tooth. I screamed: "Somebody lost a tooth in the meatloaf we're eating!" No one else found any teeth in their food and someone suggested that it may be mine. I felt around my mouth with my tongue and felt a sharp edge in the back of my mouth. The tooth that I had the root canal done on had shattered. I had never taken the time to go back to the dentist to have it capped so it was exposed the entire time. Plus, the crack and heroin that I had been doing didn't help either. I had cavities and a cracked tooth which was making eating and drinking unbearable. *This sucks!*

On top of my tooth killing me, I was having recurring pain in my private parts where my wife had attempted to emasculate me as a going away present. It wasn't until I was sober for a couple of months that I realized her bending me forcefully during our last intimate contact was no accident. I didn't want to believe she was *that* angry with me. It hurt like hell when she did it! I remember drinking and taking a lot of muscle relaxers which subdued the pain in the days following the incident. When I started to see attractive girls in meetings, it became extremely painful when I was aroused. It was a very effective means of birth control to say the least! I spent time on the computer at the downtown library in an attempt to find relief for the condition, and discovered it actually had a name: Peyronie's Disease. I read about treatment options, one being surgery. The drawback to the surgery was that there was a probability of impotence afterward. *Oh, Hell no!* Other suggestions included massive doses of Vitamin E and Lanolin in capsule form. For this to be effective it would have to have been ingested within 30-90 days of the injury. It was at least six months from the time of my injury but I was desperate for relief.

I talked with my counselor Katy about my situation and begged her to find a way for me to get Lanolin capsules. By the following week I had a script for 200 capsules and a dentist appointment to have my tooth pulled. The capsules were extremely expensive. I started taking them in massive amounts and would get very nauseous. One prescription was covered by the facility and any additional ones would have to be paid for out of pocket. There was nothing in my pockets to pay for refills so I prayed it would work. The pain eventually subsided, but I'm still disfigured. What I perceived as detrimental is actually beneficial in satisfaction, I've been told. Therefore, I would like to thank my ex wife!

My dentist appointment was with the school of dentistry; in other words, students! I had second thoughts about having my tooth pulled by rookies but I was not in a position to argue with free service. I prayed about this event too; by now, everything was in prayer! No longer praying for winning lottery tickets, TVs, money, or to get this or that back; all I wanted was God's will for me. At the appointment, two students attempted to pull out my remaining molar. One said: "Oh crap! It broke off at the root!" To which the observing dental instructor sighed and said: "Looks like we're gonna be here a bit." They asked if I had someone to drive me home and I told them that I had taken the bus. They could not sedate me without safe transport home after the procedure, and instead said they would use plenty of Novocaine. I didn't feel anything while they yanked and cut the root out, thankfully. After they were done the dental instructor said: "This is going to hurt like hell once the Novocaine wears off, so I'm prescribing Demerol and Tylenol #3s for pain." I told him that I was an addict and I couldn't take narcotics. He asked if I was sure, and I answered in the affirmative. "Then just be prepared for some severe pain. Here's a prescription for Motrin 800. Call us if there are any complications."

My mouth hurt from the extraction but not nearly as much as the self torture I endured while trying to resolve the wreckage of my past. I owed money to many people, with no way to pay them, and my wife was divorcing me. I had gotten an attorney when she filed for child support, sometime in late January or early February of 2001; I was using dope heavily at the time. My mother agreed to pay for a lawyer to represent me for the child support and visitation issue, and I would later use the same attorney for the divorce proceedings. Without knowing, I happened to choose a guy who was in the same building as my wife's attorney! I found out when I was in his office and he told me nonchalantly that he was going upstairs to speak with my wife's representation – they were buddies! He also lectured me of the evils of drug use and told me to stop before the upcoming hearings. I was lit every time I was in his office and felt like scum because I couldn't stop using. This guy didn't do a heck of a lot for me in court other than say: "My client is sorry for what he has done."

During one hearing my wife's lawyer told the judge I was a liar and couldn't be believed because I was most likely drunk and didn't remember anything. Unfortunately, I remembered everything. I wasn't drunk; was high on crack. My wife's attorney posed the question to my attorney: "Do you believe what he's saying?" My attorney answered: "I have to. He's my client." *Great, this guy's got a bunch of faith in me!* I also found out after the divorce proceedings that my attorney was also representing a lady who was divorcing her drug-addicted husband! I'm sure that didn't help.

Our divorce took place while I was sober and living at the shelter. My sponsor went with me for support and waited in the hall during the hearing. I felt empty as my wife's attorney berated me, so I practiced what I was taught in the 12 step program. I attempted to implement some halfhearted humility; there wasn't much I could contest. Her attorney portrayed me as the scum of the earth, and the domestic violence charge didn't win any points with the judge. Neither did my addictive past. Every decision was made in my wife's favor. I was ordered to pay all (including my wife's) outstanding debts; have only supervised visitation with my children; pay approximately $875 per month in child support; pay back approximately seven thousand dollars to my wife with interest; and forfeit all jointly owned furniture which she had already taken with her. The only thing left was the old freezer that used to be my grandmother's. I stood my ground fighting for a freezer that was broken and my wife didn't want anyway.

During a break in the hearing, the bailiff asked my sponsor if he knew me, and he said he did. The bailiff told my sponsor: "Tell him to stop fighting over some stupid freezer before the judge puts his ass in jail!" I respectfully conceded to the judge upon reentering the courtroom and was awarded custody of the freezer.

Along with Life Skills classes, there were classes at the shelter for money management, job search, and home management. All three courses were well needed, as I was unable to manage anything beneficial (other than copping dope) while in active addiction. They also supplied legal aid assistance to those in need, like myself. I spoke with someone regarding my debts, and he assisted with my filing for bankruptcy. What a blessing, as he walked me through the entire process.

The thought of using during all of these trials popped up. The difference, I had learned, was that I recognized that getting high wouldn't help the situation, a big change in my thought process! Using was no longer a solution to my problems. I realized the solution involved a God of my understanding, working the steps, practicing spiritual principles, and a lot of acceptance accompanied by daily surrender. I remembered to stay in the solution and not in the problem. Sometimes the best way to win the battle is to stop fighting. Tyrone E., the monitor at Orca House, asked me once: "How do you get out of a hole?" I said: "You climb out." He responded: "Yep. But first you've got to stop digging!"

CHAPTER TWENTY

Believe

I WALKED around the block every morning after breakfast and a ciga-rette, and every evening after dinner and a cigarette. This was a habit I picked up from the therapeutic walks at Orca. The block stretched from East 22nd to East 30th and encircled Cuyahoga Community College, the same school I had gone to several years earlier for my associate degree in Applied Science for Physical Therapist Assisting. The walk was med-itative and gave me a chance to get out of myself. I'd surrender all my concerns while walking and followed my breath as I walked. I'd try to turn everything over to this "higher power" everyone talked about. What better way to gain faith in a power I couldn't see than to let go and see what happened.

I knew that I couldn't do anything about seeing my kids; I was broke and they were ten hours away. I kept feeling as though I should try to make something happen but slowly I acknowledged that I was powerless over most situations in my life. The only power I did have was this God concept, and I'd go back and forth over whether or not to believe in it. Whenever something went my way then I'd credit God. If it didn't follow my desire and projected outcome then I'd be disillusioned about God.

I took a long walk one sunny day while I was missing my daughters terribly. I wandered the streets then went up to the East 55th marina. I went out onto the rocks that jutted out into Lake Erie, the ones used by people who were fishing. I was the only person, and there was a nice spring breeze coming in from Canada. I sat in the sun with my eyes closed trying to find relief from the thoughts racing in my head. I thought about how I was grateful that I was not fiending for a hit. I thought about all the things I wanted to happen: see my daughters again, find an apartment, start working.... There were many things I wanted to do, and I felt so very lost. I looked out on the lake and half-heartedly said: "If there is a God, please show me so I can believe; I don't know what else to do." I said it a few times then finally with sincerity. "Show me 'cause I'm lost." I looked down at the rocks and felt even more lost. I heard a small buzzing which became increasingly louder. It sounded like a bumblebee. I looked up and the largest bee I had ever seen was hovering in front of me! I could feel the air from its' wings! I waved my hands thinking that if I got one good shot, I'd knock it into the lake without getting stung. I stood up on the rocks waving at the thing screaming: "Bee...leave," with every swat. "Bee... leave, bee...leave, bee-leave....BELIEVE!" Chills ran up my spine, the hair stood up on the back of my neck and tears rolled down my cheeks. I was given my answer. That was how I came to *believe* in a power greater than myself.

I BEGAN to live life in 15 hour shifts: up by 8 a.m. for breakfast, and in my bunk by 11 p.m. weekdays. I was actually adjusting to a sleep schedule, and was in my bunk reading before going to sleep nightly. The morning of September 11, 2001 started out like any other morning. I woke up and kneeled beside my bunk to pray, no longer self conscious about it. After prayer I'd go to the bathroom, then down the hall to breakfast, available between 6:30 and 8:30 a.m. and consisting of dry cereal and milk on weekdays. An occasional honey bun would find its' way to the table.

As I walked past the wide screen TV in the dining hall, a number of guys were standing there saying: "Did you see that shit?!" They said a plane ran into one of the twin towers in New York. I stood there watching the TV and witnessed the second plane hit a tower. We said: "What was that?" It was like a movie.

The director of the facility came out of his office and said the Salvation Army was beginning to mobilize. The local news cut in and said most state and federal offices were closing downtown, and they started telling people to stay home. The facility I was in was on East 22nd in downtown Cleveland. I decided to walk further downtown to see what was up. People were freaking out, and many folks stopped their cars and were standing in the street. It was like *The Twilight Zone!* As I was walking, a large plane flew overhead. It was extremely low and loud as hell. I would later find out that this was one of the hijacked planes. I went back to the shelter and continued to watch the news. As the morning progressed we witnessed the eventual crumble of both towers, a plane ramming the Pentagon and another diverted plane (the one that had flown over my head) crash in a field somewhere in Pennsylvania. The day was dedicated to prayer and confusion.

As the days passed, donations of water bottles and non perishable food piled into our facility. We volunteered to load the trucks that would take the supplies to Ground Zero. Once again, I felt as though I was part of something much greater than myself; the common goal had adjusted my dim view of humanity. I saw all types of people, colors, races and genders bond to help others. It was similar to recovering men and women helping one another stay clean and sober for our mutual benefit and preservation. The widespread alliance of an altruistic restoration of ourselves. I began to recognize, if but for a short time, one people and one race: the human race. It reminded me of the Jamaican motto: "Out of many, one people." I witnessed man's inhumanity to his fellow man on the morning, noon and nightly news. Could this togetherness in time of peril be "Love Thy Neighbor" and "Do unto others as you would have them do unto you" that I'd heard about but had rarely come across?

I had arrived at the shelter in July, 2001. By Christmas, at least three people had come and gone from the relapse bunk in our room. One guy left the same day he'd arrived. Some focus on finding a job rather than getting a firm foundation in sobriety first. Those are the guys who'd equate work with success, and forgot the hopeless state of mind and spiritual bankruptcy of their last days of using. A job will not keep me sober, a girlfriend will not keep me clean and a car will not maintain my recovery from drugs, alcohol and a life that is unmanageable. However, these "things" add to the illusion of stability while in actuality, my insides were full of low self-esteem and a thousand forms of fear. I had to work on my insides. I'd had a history of trying to fix the outside first, then wondering how I'd lost the job, the girl, and the car. If I didn't have a solid defense against the first hit, then *I'm hit!* My insides had to match my outsides. Tyrone E. would say: "You can put a suit on a pig but it's still a pig. The only thing that has changed is what he's wearing."

Seeing the revolving sobriety bunk firsthand reinforced my commitment to living a clean and sober lifestyle. I continued going to meetings and kept in contact with my sponsor. I started sitting in with my sponsor to watch him take other guys through the steps. The more I worked with and assisted my sponsor, the more I gained a working knowledge of the 12 step program. I was told that I should start sponsoring, which scared the crap out of me. Tyrone E.'s words echoed in my head: "You gotta give it away to keep it," and, "There's nothing more selfish than getting what was freely given to you and not giving it away."

I started to feel and exhibit more confidence in my daily activities, at least I thought so, and it was time to start working. I'd learned to ask God first for direction, then run it by someone else before acting upon it. It was amazing that when I wanted something or thought something was best for me, God's voice sounded a lot like my voice and gave me the OK! "If you grade your own paper every time then you'll always get an A," words of wisdom from Tyrone E.

I ran my thoughts past my counselor and my sponsor. I needed objective views from supportive, experienced, non biased colleagues in recovery. Also, I was reminded that God speaks through people. Katy told me that she had been watching me and thought I should start off with something part-time so that I could ease my way back into the workforce. She asked: "What did your sponsor say?" I told her I'd let her know as soon as I asked him. I went to my sponsor and he told me that I had to start living what I'd learned. He asked: "What did your counselor say?" I told him about working part-time. "Go for it!" he said.

The last time I worked was in early 1999 and that was sporadic, at best. It was now late 2001 and I was laying in my bunk searching through classified ads. I was last employed as a licensed physical therapist assistant, but had reservations about going back primarily because of the domestic violence charge against me, so I decided to look for something less restrictive. I was scared of being rejected and looked down upon.

I started circling jobs that worked during third shift, as there were plenty of factory and warehouse jobs available. There was one ad for a physical therapist assistant, part-time, in home health. I circled the ad but was positive I wouldn't be applying for it. I took the want ads to Katy to show her the jobs for which I would apply.

"You don't need to be working third shift," Katy said. "You need to work a schedule conducive to your newly formed sleep pattern; not in the middle of the night." She pointed to the part-time therapist job. I cringed, telling her that they might not hire me. "How do you know unless you apply?" *Crap!* I didn't want to hear that. "It's part-time, you're trained in that field, and it's during the day. Step out on faith and make the effort. That's what recovery is about; taking the action and leaving the results in God's hands."

If I was to stay plugged into this recovery thing I had to start living by spiritual principles, one of which was courage. I had to have the courage to step out on faith and see what happened. Nothing happens unless I take the action first. I heard Tyrone E. in my head: "Faith has feet!" Something else I'd heard in the rooms of recovery: If I'm sitting at the kitchen table praying for something to eat then I'll most likely starve if I don't get up from the table and take the steps to get some food. God will not send a pizza directly to me. I have to get up and order it! My sponsor shared an acronym for FAITH: Father Always In Thy Hands.

I called the number regarding the physical therapist assistant job, and was asked when I would be able to come in for an interview. *Damn! This is happening much too quickly!* The voice on the phone: "How about tomorrow at 1 p.m.?" Although I wanted to say *How about next week some-*

time? I said, "Tomorrow is fine." *Where the hell did that come from?!*

I pulled together a half-assed resume with a two year gap in my work history. *It should be interesting trying to explain this shit!* Scenarios coursed through my head. *Do I tell them about my record? Do I tell them I live in a homeless shelter? Do I tell them I'm a recovered addict and alcoholic?* I was up early the next day on my knees praying for direction and strength. I ate breakfast, smoked a cigarette and went on my daily morning walk around the block. During the walk I kept repeating: "Thy will be done."

I borrowed a tie from one of my roommates and prepared for the inevitable. The interview was half an hour away in Willoughby, and my car was at my mother's house. I took a bus to my mom's and borrowed her car to go to the interview, worrying the entire time about what I was going to say. I made it to the interview by 12:30 and sat in the parking lot smoking one cigarette after another.

Twenty minutes later, I got out of the car, said a prayer, and walked into the building. I gave the receptionist my name and said I was there for an interview. She said they were expecting me. *Oh God!* She handed me an application for employment and asked me to complete it. My hands were shaking as I tried to print my name. The segment on the application that asked: Have you ever been arrested and if so, please explain. *Oh shit! What do I do?* Just as soon as I asked myself this question I answered it: Tell the truth. This had been the answer all along.

I handed the completed application to the secretary and she told me to have a seat. I recited the Serenity Prayer over and over again in my head. I had decided to answer truthfully any question that was asked. The owner of the company entered, shook my hand and escorted me into an office. She had built the company from the ground up, and I was impressed. After reviewing my resume, she asked about the arrest, as I had knew she would. I told her everything and some things she didn't even ask about! It was like I was in confession or something, as I wanted her to know everything about me. In some way, I thought I would scare her away if she knew my story, but she seemed more interested than offended. Surprisingly enough, she offered me the job! She said she was impressed by my honesty. I sure didn't see that coming!

I had been receiving letters from CSEA (Child Support Enforcement Agency) since I arrived at the shelter. Both my sponsor and counselor encouraged me to work on myself first before focusing on employment immediately. I knew that if I didn't have a firm foundation in recovery before I got a job, then I might be off and running when I got my first paycheck. I'd have time to pay the arrearages that were piling up as soon as I got a job. I contacted the child support agency to let them know that I was working, and gave them the information they needed to start collecting from my paycheck. I was left with very little after each check but, I was learning to be responsible.

Time rocked on and eventually I was given an opportunity to work full-time. I gave my paychecks to my counselor, who opened up a savings account for me. I kept just enough money for cigarettes and gas for my car. I didn't need money for anything else as food and shelter were provided. It wasn't like I was dating anybody either. What was I going to say to my date anyway? "Hey, you want to come back to the shelter with me and hang out in my bunk for awhile, baby?"

I was permitted to park my car at the shelter since I had to use it for work, and by February of 2002, I had saved approximately $900! I asked my sponsor if he thought I was ready to move from the shelter. "What does your counselor think?" he asked. *Deja vu.* I asked my counselor and she said I was ready to give my bed up to someone who needed it like I did when I arrived. And then: "What did your sponsor say?"

"He said to ask you!"

"You've learned to ask for help," she said, "you've learned to follow directions, you have the 12 steps, you have a support group, a homegroup and a God of your understanding...start looking for your new home."

I was ready to put this recovery thing to the test, as I looked through the paper. I found an efficiency on the westside of Cleveland in Lakewood, in an eight storey apartment building called Lake House, one of many lining Lake Erie. I set up an appointment with the owner, Tim, a young guy who owned a few rentals in the area. The rent was $325 per month, and the apartment was on the second floor. There was a small kitchen with a mini fridge, a larger room, a door that separated the walk-in closet, and a bathroom next to it. The place was perfect! Fear rushed over me when I filled out the application, as my work and credit history sucked, and I had recently filed for bankruptcy. I knew that wouldn't look very pleasing to a new landlord. All I could do was pray and continue doing the right thing no matter what.

A week lapsed before I heard back. Tim offered me the apartment! I didn't expect to get the place, but he said he wanted to help me out. After receiving the terrific news, all I could think about was not having to smell farts and feet every night. That was enough to celebrate in and of itself!

CHAPTER TWENTY-ONE

Apartment Living

I PACKED my belongings for the move. I had accumulated a lot of books on recovery and spiritual material while living at PASS, and had acquired some new/pre-owned clothing from the donation bins. I found it hard to believe I was leaving a sober living environment. I had been at PASS for a little more than eight months, and at Orca House for 104 days prior to that. In total, I was in treatment and sober living just shy of one year.

The Salvation Army assisted in the move by furnishing a new single mattress and box spring, a blue wool blanket, broom and dust pan and cleaning supplies for which I was grateful. I found a small glass table for five bucks. My mom went to a thrift store and purchased my kitchen utensils, and hooked me up with a small microwave oven. A couple of my friends from the shelter used the Salvation Army truck to help me move. It took about 15 minutes to move everything in, and the guys congratulated me on finding such a nice place. They told me not to forget how I got there and what I needed to do to stay sober.

I closed the door as they left and turned around to look at my new place. I had a box spring and mattress in the middle of the bedroom/living room, my tiny glass table next to it and some stuff sitting on the counter of the kitchen which was also part of the living room and bedroom. I stood there and cried by myself for a minute or two. I was happy and thankful reflecting on the past couple of years of my life. I had learned to be grateful for what I had at this moment. I thought back to when I had the family, hot tub, house and all the material crap that made me feel successful. At that time, all I needed to do to feel good about myself was to buy more shit. The more shit the more secure and accomplished I imagined myself to be. So when I lost all that crap I felt worthless because I had put my self worth in "things." I was happier than I had ever been with just a mattress on the floor in a one room apartment to which I had the key. I was learning that it was not about how much I had; it was more about appreciating what I have that elicited true happiness and humility.

During the next few days I tried to adjust to my new independence and surroundings. The first thing I did was to locate a 12 step meeting. I found one on Sunday nights at Cove Church, within walking distance of my apartment, and continued to hit my regular meetings on the eastside. The apartment did not permit smoking, so every time I wanted a cigarette I had to go outside the main lobby of the building. I really wanted to stop smoking, as my lungs were shot from years of smoking various combustible materials. Nothing like sucking in hot smoke and holding it in your lungs to ravage the 'ol pulmonary system. I hit the stem so hard in active addiction that the hot choy (screen) would fly into my mouth and burn my tongue. I'd just spit it out and reload. Plus, there were numerous times I inhaled the dope itself by hitting it too hard. Although my lungs eventually numbed out when smoking crack they were damaged just the same. I had been coughing up gobs of pitch black sputum every morning for the past year or so, and it was getting difficult to walk any distance without having shortness of breath. It didn't help matters that I had asthma, though the symptoms weren't that bad when I was smoking rock. However, I don't endorse its use as a bronchial dilator!

I continued to settle into a regimen: Up at 6 a.m. weekdays to pray, read my 24 hour and Just For Today meditation books, eat breakfast, take a 1-2 mile therapeutic walk, go home to shower, then head off to work. After work I would eat, go to a meeting then home, read recovery literature, say prayers and go to bed. On weekends I'd perform the same morning ritual but then go to my mother's home where she made dinner Saturdays and Sundays to try to fatten me up. I'd take my recovery and spiritual literature with me to read. I had gotten into the habit of not watching a lot of TV, and I'd spend the night in the same guest room that I use to get high in before I went to Orca for treatment. While I was gone, my mom had thrown away every "get high" utensil she could find in there and opened the drapes to let the sun in. It had an entirely different vibe. When I was using it felt lifeless, dark and empty. Now, it felt like a guest room and I was a welcomed guest. I picked up my acoustic guitar and started to relearn some songs. After Sunday dinner, my mom packed up all the leftovers and sent them home with me so I'd have something to eat during the week. I'd then drive back to the westside in time for my 8 o'clock meeting at the church.

One day I got a call from Tyrone S. I hadn't seen or heard from him in over a year, and thought he had gone back to using like a couple of other guys I had run into from Orca. He heard that I was still doing the recovery thing and wanted to talk to me. He was also living on the westside, on West 102nd off Detroit.

It was great to see Ty again. As I walked into his apartment I noticed he had his living room window propped open with his Big Book of *Alcoholics Anonymous*. He had a small one bedroom, a little hoopty (car) and a girlfriend. He said he wasn't very happy, and the apartment sucked because the dope dealers would come out at night to serve by his window. They asked him regularly, "Are you straight?" meaning, did he want anything. He said his hoopty was on its last legs and his current girlfriend smoked dope in the bathroom. At times he felt like smoking with her.

Tyrone had stopped going to meetings for awhile. He had gotten a sponsor when he got out of Orca but stopped when he got his "life together." I reminded him what we had promised one another at Orca: We were going to be the two out of 16 that stayed clean. He mumbled that he remembered. I told him that I was his new sponsor, as I knew this would not only help me stay sober but would benefit Ty too.

Tyrone and I started hitting meetings together. We went to so many that when we didn't show up together someone would ask: "Where's your partner?" I took Ty through his first three steps in my apartment and got him started on his fourth step inventory. I followed the procedure that my sponsor used with me and his sponsor used with him. Passed on from sponsor to sponsee. Within the next few months Tyrone had completed the 12 steps and had a working knowledge of them as well. Shortly after completing the steps Tyrone disappeared. He stopped calling and his phone was cut off. I drove by his old apartment but no one answered the door. My worst fear was that he had gone back out. I didn't hear from Tyrone again for nearly a year.

WITHIN THE first few months of apartment life, supervised visitation was awarded to me by the court. The restraining orders were removed and I was allowed within 500 feet of my daughters and ex-wife. I contacted my ex in South Carolina and planned a visit. I had seen them prior to this in a court setting for about 10-15 minutes. It had been more than a year since I hugged my little girls. I was extremely happy about seeing them but terrified with the reality of having my ex oversee the visit. I knew that if she got pissed at me for any reason, justified or not, I would most likely lose visitation privileges and very possibly wind up with a case! I planned for the 10 hour drive by packing my Big Book, 24 Hour a Day book, the N.A. Basic Text and a bag full of cassettes on recovery for the journey.

I was scared to be face to face with my ex again, I told my sponsor, and still harbored some ill will toward her for taking the girls and for attempting to emasculate me. I did not trust her. My sponsor reminded me that I had given her reason not to trust me due to my drinking and drugging. He said that this would be a good time to make my 9th step face to face amends to her. I told him that I had done that at Orca house. Shortly after I arrived at Orca my counselor called my ex, and I was allowed to speak with her for a minute. I told her that I had forgiven her for what she had done. She said: "What?! You forgive me? You're crazy!" and hung up the phone. My sponsor explained that this was not the amends process but more like denial and justification on my part. I had to agree with him. He said it was time to clean my side of the street, not hers.

My mother lent me money and her car for the trip to South Carolina. Dozens of scenarios ran through my head during the drive. When I stopped at rest areas, I prayed for strength, guidance and wisdom to do the right thing. I listened to recovery tapes the entire way and recited mentally that my primary purpose was to stay sober. I surrendered repeatedly to my Higher Power every time I started to shake with the fear of expectation. I continually reminded myself that whatever was about to happen it couldn't be worse than losing myself and soul to dope and alcohol. While watching the sun set through the hills and valleys of West Virginia I recited: "If God is for me then who could be against me?" and, "The Lord is my light and my salvation, whom shall I fear?" Both were my mantras for the rest of the trip. I had to admit my powerlessness over the situation and allow a new power in. I had to let go in order to receive.

PART III
CHAPTER TWENTY-TWO

My Girls

IT WAS WARM and humid when I arrived in South Carolina, ten hours on I-77 south all the way to Columbia. Prior to my arrival, my ex told me I could sleep on their couch for the weekend I was there. When I got there, however, she said her father didn't think it was a good idea. It was cool with me because I was stressed about being in the same environment with her. My daughters were the ones who really wanted me to stay there, not her. When I arrived, the girls ran up to me screaming "Daddy!" I flashed back to happier times when we were all together as a family, but it was extremely awkward now.

In the back of my head I knew that we would never be a family like before. It was a bittersweet reunion and I was determined to make the best of it. I felt out of place. Although I felt uneasy around my ex, we did have history together. I had mixed feelings. I trusted her completely when we were married, and then didn't when she took the girls. Now I wasn't sure. A multitude of emotions were pulling at me. I suggested we go to dinner together after I got a motel room. I wanted to remove myself from the situation temporarily so I could sort out what I was feeling.

For so many years I had masked my feelings with drugs and alcohol. When I went into treatment at Orca the only two things I felt were fear and anger. Plus my reactions to all situations were fear based and often violent. If I thought I was going to lose something (I thought I deserved) I would fight to hold onto it, and if I thought I wasn't going to get something (that I felt I deserved) I'd fight to get it. I was totally self-centered. I didn't know that I could make choices in how I responded to situations. I'd learned to identify states of confusion, anxiety, insecurity, inferiority and others. All these and more overwhelmed me. My old solution to this type of situation was to be silent and expect others to figure out why I was quiet (passively giving me control) or start yelling in order to keep everyone at bay so I could feel as though I had some control over things. I had to sort it out. I was given a suggestion about where to look for an inexpensive motel. I gave the girls a hug and told them I'd call as soon as I was settled. They wanted to go with me but my ex said no. I really needed some time alone.

I checked into a motel a couple of miles away, called my sponsor and told him how I was feeling. Just being able to express what was going around in my head was a relief. My brain tended to go straight to worst case scenarios if I dwelled on something long enough. Hopelessness and self-pity would kick in, then spiral down into guilt and remorse. Before I knew it there could be plenty of fertile ground to plant a seed of doubt in my sobriety; the perfect set up to spark a relapse. Thank God I had some-one to talk to who listened and understood. The more I shared, the more readily a solution usually presented itself. The solution to this dilemma manifested too. The solution was to trust God, be respectful and open minded, refrain from judgment and try to be the best father that I could be. Not for the rest of my visit, not for the rest of my life, just for the rest of the day. Tomorrow was another day. The wise words of my sponsor which I carried with me during times of affliction: "Do what you can and not what you can't."

My first supervised weekend with my daughters ended soon after it started. Our last outing before my departure was a visit to a go-cart track/video game parlor. My four-year-old daughter got in a go-cart with me and my oldest daughter, nine-years-old, drove her own. It was the first time all weekend that we were somewhat away from the supervision of my ex. We raced each other while she was busy talking on her phone. After a few times around the track we played video games and took some pictures in the photo booth. I struggled to maintain a happy face and not burst out crying. I was scheduled to leave after our outing Saturday eve-ning after having arrived Friday afternoon. I was beginning to lose it. I loved them so much that it felt as though my heart was breaking the more

I hugged them.

It was getting dark by the time we pulled up to their home, and I went inside to say goodbye. I asked my ex if she would take a couple of pictures of me with the girls and she agreed. Then she sent them to put on their pajamas. My oldest asked if I would tuck her in as I did nightly when they lived in Cleveland. I asked my ex if it was okay, and she agreed to that as well. While the girls were putting on their pajamas, my ex and I had a quick second to talk. I asked her why she left me and she replied: "Oh Dave, let's not get into that!" I felt a churning in my stomach and I began to shake slightly.

My mindset at the time was that nothing could justify leaving me and especially taking the kids too. I had believed marriage to be a forever deal. Self-pity and anger started to build. When we lived together and I got angry, I would usually stomp around, wave my hands and yell. I knew I had to choose another option this time or I could wind up in a South Carolina jail for the evening! I backed myself up to the dining room wall and put my hands behind my back so the pressure of leaning on them would keep them in place. I didn't trust myself. It was all I could do to stay in one place and speak in a calm albeit somewhat shaky voice.

Fortunately my two little girls ran into the room wearing their pajamas and announced: "We're ready for you to tuck us in, Daddy!" *Thank God!* I walked into a bedroom and lay down on the bed between them. I read a couple of pages to them from a children's book. A few minutes went by and my ex said: "It's time to go to bed. Your daddy has a long ride ahead of him." We said prayers together, I kissed the youngest on the head and told her she was getting to be a big girl. She said: "Goodnight, Daddy." I carried my oldest on my back into her room. We both kneeled down and said prayers again. She asked if I would be back soon, and I told her I would visit again as soon as possible. She hugged me and wouldn't let go. Her mother told her repeatedly that it was bedtime and I had to leave. I told my daughter I loved her and that I really enjoyed seeing both she and her sister. I left the room and she called me back in for another hug. Her mother said: "Your father has to leave now." Tears were building up in my eyes as I walked out of her room again. She called to me one more time: "Daddy, one more thing I have to tell you!" Her mother said: "One more thing and that's it!" I walked back in and sat next to her on her bed. She looked directly in my eyes and said: "Daddy, I just wanted you to know that I'm happy that you're not doing drugs anymore." I couldn't hold back the tears any longer. I started crying, hugged her and said: "I'm happy too, sweetheart."

One of the most difficult things that I ever had to do was to leave her room that night. As I walked out the front door I kept my head turned away from my ex, as I didn't want her to see how shaken up I was. She told me to drive safely and then closed the front door. I got into my car and pulled out of the housing complex onto the main road. I couldn't see the road for the tears. I pulled into a Piggly Wiggly parking lot and sobbed uncontrollably for about twenty minutes. I felt so alone. Although the emotional pain of self-pity and abandonment ripped at me, the thought of picking up a drink or a drug never crossed my mind.

Trips to South Carolina became more frequent and eventually I was awarded unsupervised visitation. I called the Columbia, South Carolina central office of Alcoholics Anonymous and made sure that I attended meetings while in town. It was like an oasis: I was able to bond with out-of-state alkies! Their support and encouragement helped me through many a weekend of emotional turmoil. My daughters started to visit me too. Their mother and I each agreed to drive to Virginia, half way between Cleveland and Columbia, where we would exchange the children. Two young girls and a father staying in an efficiency apartment with one bathroom was educational! I had a queen-sized bed and a daybed. We would always wind up sleeping together in the queen; six arms and six legs fighting for the most comfortable sleeping position. Fortunately, we were able to visit my mother for good home-cooked meals and room to stretch our legs.

As the girls have gotten older, we see less of each other. My youngest daughter, a teenager, banned me from visiting her for Halloween a few years ago and my adult daughter is busy with college and work. I totally regret the years away from them when they were younger. The thought of moving to South Carolina to be closer to them crossed my mind a few times in early sobriety. It was always offset by focusing on a solid foundation in recovery. I had learned to put my recovery first above everything, even if it meant losing my children. Had I not made sobriety my priority then I would certainly not have been able to withstand the shit storms that came and went. Recovery required full time participation. It was not something to do just on weekends or a few times a week. I was committed to getting high everyday so it only made sense to put as much if not more effort in staying clean a day at a time.

CHAPTER TWENTY-THREE

Meditation in Motion

TYRONE CALLED ME one day out of the blue; I had not heard from him for more than six months. He had been in the hospital and was on a feeding tube. Tyrone had a biopsy taken from his lungs and in the process, his esophagus had been punctured. He was unable to eat solid food for months and had lost a great deal of weight. The doctors found cancerous cells and removed a few nodules. He said he was okay, and raved about a woman who came into his hospital room daily to pray with him. He called her an angel, as she encouraged his spirit and allowed him to convalesce at her home.

Within a year or so of meeting her, I was the best man at their wedding. No one had ever asked me to be best anything before! It was an honor.

I told Tyrone that we needed to attend some meetings together, and he agreed. "After they get this tube out of me, it's on!" he said. The feeding tube was eventually removed and we began hitting meetings together with a passion. It was during this time that my mother called to inform me that she was scheduled to have open heart surgery.

My mom had been going back and forth to the cardiologist for a few years due to erratic heartbeats and fatigue. One time, years before, my oldest daughter and my mother went to the bank together. My mom passed out and fell face first onto the pavement breaking her wrist. Fortunately my seven-year-old was calm enough to give her phone number and the police contacted my wife and me. I found out later that my mother's occasional dizziness and blackouts were heart-related. All kinds of scenarios ran through my head thinking about the upcoming surgery.

Around the same time, my friend and monitor from Orca House, Tyrone E., had died. He had been on the list for a liver transplant but, unfortunately, it didn't materialize for him. He was the first guy I shared all of my addictive emotional baggage with; the first person who gave me hope that I could get clean; the person who suggested I go to further treatment; the guy with the endless recovery mantras. I couldn't believe he was gone. The first time my mother came to visit me at Orca, Tyrone was the monitor at the front desk. After she left Tyrone asked: "Was that your mother, Smeltz?" I nodded. "That woman has a lot of class...you can tell!" I thanked him and felt important for a few minutes, albeit, through a compliment given to my mother.

The funeral for Tyrone E. was in June or July. Coincidentally my youngest flew into Cleveland the same day to begin her summer visit. I picked her up from the airport and told her that Tyrone at Orca had died and we were on our way to his funeral. She didn't expect that! She was only seven when she met Tyrone at the Friday Orca alumni meeting. When Tyrone met her, he asked: "Is this the little girl you thought you'd never see again?" I nodded and smiled. "I told you miracles happen in recovery." As we viewed Tyrone's body for the last time I could almost hear him break off a final thought-provoking morsel of recovery which he'd expressed to me and has always stayed with me. "There's a pair of pajamas in detox that will fit any length of sobriety!" Classic Tyronism! Thanks for your help, Tyrone E. You'll never know how much your words and kindness sparked my recovery. I miss you.

My mother's heart surgery was performed without complication. A valve was replaced, a pacemaker inserted, and the doctor sewed up a hole in her heart that he believed to be genetic. Seeing my mother in the recovery room after surgery was difficult. She was in a lot of pain and highly med-icated. I was glad to be there with her while I was in a sober state. There had been a time, while in active addiction, that I took my mom to Kaiser urgent care because she complained about severe shortness of breath and nausea. I sat next to her while she lay on the gurney. The attending phy-sician had left the room momentarily leaving me alone with my mom. I was fiending like crazy at the time. I was feeling dope sick and knew if I could get a hit of crack I'd be okay enough to sit there for another hour without jumping out of my skin. We were on Cedar Road where I had copped many a time before. I was sitting on the edge of my seat staring at my mother's purse. Her eyes were closed, face contorted in pain. I stood up, slowly backed over to her purse, and took out her wallet. She had about $15, so I took out ten. I closed the wallet and started to put it back in her purse when a nurse walked around the drape and saw me. She looked at my mom and saw her eyes were closed. Then she looked at me, shook her head and started an I.V. line on my mother. I told her to tell my mom I'd be right back., scurried out of the ER, and into her car.

I drove down Cedar and spotted a young dope boy hanging out. I gave him the nod and he came over to the car. I told him I needed a ten. He walked down around a building, came back and put a piece in my hand. By this point in the game I always had a stem or some kind of shooter on me so I could smoke at a moment's notice. I pulled around the corner off the main street and loaded my stem. I started to heat up the stem but the dope wasn't melting. I put the flame to the end of the stem to light it directly. Still nothing. I tried and tried but eventually the stem was too hot to hold or hit. It was a dummy! This guy took my – actually my mother's – $10 and sold me a dummy. In my smoking career I had tried to light up everything from plaster to bits of soap and swore it had to be dope. I didn't have any more money and was feeling guilty for not only stealing from my mother, but for doing it while she was ill. I had to get back to the ER, and was feeling like pure shit! I'll never forget the remorse, guilt and self-hatred I felt. I never want to forget how I lived and what I had become.

As I stood next to my mother's bed, holding her hand after her heart surgery, I thanked God for taking away the obsession to use. I was grateful and humbled.

My mother recuperated from surgery at the Cleveland Clinic for roughly a week, then went to a rehab facility for a month. I valued the importance of integrating the body, mind and spirit as a way of treating the whole person. My mom's recovery reminded me that my body was a temple. She had been an avid practitioner of Tai Chi Chuan prior to and post surgery. She trained with her senior friends at the Jewish Community Center and Lyndhurst senior center, and her consistent participation in the art may have played a large part in her healing. While in rehab, she showed everyone Tai Chi moves. She had the opportunity to go to China shortly after her discharge, and said she was the only black woman up at 5 a.m. in Beijing doing the 24 Yang Style form with the Chinese. She said she freaked 'em out!

I knew that not only was it important not to pick up any mood or mind altering substances, but that I needed to get better physically, mentally and spiritually, as well. My first year out of treatment I had asked a monitor, Chris, if he knew of anyone teaching Tai Chi or karate, as Chris was an ex golden gloves. My initial motivation for wanting to learn martial arts was to be able to defend myself if needed, as you never knew when a sponsee might flip the script and become violent. I had seen it happen before at a meeting and I wanted to be prepared.

I would later find martial arts to be meditation in motion. It was a great way to learn discipline and focus. Chris told me about an older black gentleman who could fight six people at once and was a master in kung fu: Grandmaster Arthur E. Sikes. I learned that Grandmaster Sikes held a master 5th degree black belt in karate as well as a master 4th degree in kung fu awarded to him from his teacher, the great Grandmaster Willem Reeders. I had to meet this dude!

Chris took me to meet Grandmaster at the Martin Luther King recreation center on Shaw Avenue where he was teaching martial arts classes. Chris introduced me as a recovering friend who wanted to learn self-defense, having had no prior experience in the arts. I watched the guys on the floor to see if it was something I might be interested in doing. I was standing on the side of the gym watching these men of color put one another to the floor, into submission holds, and some really cool stuff that reminded me of Bruce Lee on the '70s TV show *The Green Hornet*. Only this time it wasn't choreographed! It didn't take long to decide. I asked when I could start and he told me to get out on the floor. *Holy shit!*

I trained with Grandmaster Sikes for five years and still train with Pastor Robert Edmonds, a First Degree Red Sash Master in the art of Liu Seong Gung Fu and Kuntao, as recognized and awarded by Grandmaster Sikes. I met Rob the first day of training, and he was patient with me while most of the other students used me as a practice dummy. Grandmaster was patient with me, as well. I think he tolerated me those first few months as a favor to Chris.

I learned many things from Grandmaster that enhanced my sobriety and ability to live by spiritual principles. One of the gems of wisdom he shared with us while training had to do with patience and focus. While performing techniques in self-defense I tried to initiate the movement as fast as I could, as I'd seen guys in Kung Fu movies use lightning speed to have their opponent on the ground in seconds. That's what I thought it was about. Grandmaster said: "This ain't the movies; it's self-defense!" Then: "If you can't do it slow then you can't do it fast!" He explained that we should be able to perform a technique accurately and make it work no matter how fast we moved. When it was done slowly, all of the nuances within the technique were visible. Performing each of them with precision guaranteed successful completion every time, no matter the situation. It takes individual steps to reach a destination.

Grandmaster greeted and departed us with both hands pressed together in front of his chest with a slight bow. This gesture, I learned, was used as a sign of greeting, gratitude, and reverence. Grandmaster also used it as a sign of apology after accidentally hitting us during a demonstration or technique. I would later find out that this gesture is also associated with the Sanskrit word, Namaste, which literally means "I bow to you." It is also used as a greeting or acknowledgement of the equality of all, and pays honor to the sacredness of all. Later, when studying Zen Buddhist beliefs, I recognized the same gesture, referred to as "Gassho."

Other benefits of martial arts included mindfulness and persever-ance. Being able to concentrate on one thing at a time is a valuable asset to recovery. While a student of Grandmaster's, I learned to concentrate on one thing or action at a time. During active addiction, I always had 10,000 thoughts racing through my head: *Where am I gonna get money to cop? I hope the dude doesn't rip me off. Do my kids think about me? I can't believe she left me. How do I stop using drugs?* A constant barrage that followed me into recovery as well: *Does this sobriety thing work? If I do get sober can I stay sober? Why is this dude at the table giving me a dirty look? I hope they don't pick me for anything. I can't let anybody know I'm scared. I really hurt my mother. I really hurt my kids. What's my wife doing? Will I see my family again?*

I found that the more I thought about the past and the future, the past and future made up every waking moment. It was like living on autopi-lot with emotional upheaval induced by identification with thoughts and memories. I was so consumed by what happened and what might happen that my "now" was made up of things and situations that didn't exist any-more or things and situations that hadn't, or possibly wouldn't, happen. While performing martial art techniques repeatedly, I learned persever-ance in conjunction with mindfulness. To think of anything other than the technique I was performing would create a distraction. I was learning to acknowledge the discursive thoughts and not attach to them. The more I attached myself to thoughts or feelings, the more I divided my power and energy.

Early in sobriety at Orca, I was sitting by the window in the dining/group therapy room, and my attention was all over the place: every siren from a passing EMS truck, every horn blowing and every girl walking past the window deserved my concern. It didn't take much to take the focus off the present situation. It was much easier to allow myself to be distract-ed when I was uncomfortable being with me in the present moment. If I don't like me then why would I want to be with me? Especially alone! The best way to divert attention from the present moment without the convenience of drugs or alcohol is by welcoming chaos and confusion. I had become a master at fooling myself; the truth was too painful. Rationalization and justification kept me stuck on stupid and locked on dumb. Another Tyronism: "Rationalization and justification are like masturbation: you're only fucking *yourself!*"

Grandmaster Sikes introduced me to meditation. Up until this point, I would practice my 11th step meditation by focusing on something I had read regarding recovery or a scripture verse. This was more contemplation than meditation, I later learned. Grandmaster told me to focus on my breath only and not on thoughts; I had to empty my mind and that was no small task! I began to sit for five minutes at a time, as that was all I could handle. It was very difficult to shift my awareness from thought. I'd start thinking of things said to me earlier in the day, and would always think about my children. I had a dialogue with imaginary people and imagined scenarios of past and future events. On occasion, I was able to rest those thoughts and that was when reggae bass lines started popping off! And then colors and images. All the time, I would attempt to redirect my focus back to the breath. I began my five minute sits every morning after prayer and every evening before going to sleep. Initially this practice helped me learn to just sit still, an option I never knew existed. Just being, and learning to be alright with being. It was an introduction to someone I'd never met before: Me.

During my period of training with Grandmaster Sikes, my close friend and sponsee, Tyrone S., became more available following his recent hospitalization. Tyrone and I started an A.A. meeting, New Direction, at the old Cleveland Rehab facility for alcoholics with emotional and mental disorders. Every Wednesday at 7:30 we met and facilitated a discussion group. Many of the residents became like family and the time spent there certainly helped strengthen our sobriety. We also got into a detox facility at the Salvation Army, sharing our experience, strength and hope with men and women attempting to detox from drugs and/or alcohol. We were doing 12 step work by carrying the message of recovery and reinforcing our recovery as well. Tyrone and I continued to go to meetings together including my homegroup, Listen To Learn, which he joined too. We hit meetings on the east- and westside of Cleveland on a regular basis, always looking for different ones to visit. We made yearly visits to Founders Day in Akron, sponsoring and co-sponsoring many. I sponsored Tyrone on his first spiritual retreat. My sponsor introduced me to my first one so I passed the experience on to Ty. He, in turn, passed it to one of his sponsees. My whole life in recovery was catapulted into a new understanding and appreciation for sobriety after I attended. I wanted this for Tyrone also, as we shared a close bond with one another. This period of vigorous 12 step work would soon serve as a solid foundation to sustain me through the trials and tribulations forthcoming.

CHAPTER TWENTY-FOUR

Thy Will Be Done

I RECEIVED a call from my mother. She had been making frequent trips to her cardiologist following surgery. She informed me that she had been diagnosed with congestive heart failure, and amyloidosis of the heart. It carried a terminal prognosis: approximately six months. I had trouble responding to the news. My mother asked if I was okay. I asked if she was okay. There was silence. We spoke without words.

I had heard of congestive heart failure but not amyloidosis. My mother had the symptoms of both maladies, and she was unable to lay supine for the past few years. She had become accustomed to sleeping upright in bed with pillows behind her so that she could breathe comfortably. It was becoming more and more difficult for her to walk any distance without becoming greatly fatigued. I had moved back to the eastside from Lakewood into an apartment building owned by my friend and I-Tal bass player, Dave Valentine. He allowed me to rent month-to-month, which was a blessing because I didn't know how long my mother would be able to continue to function independently. I lived ten minutes from her house and could be there at a moment's notice.

For years, my mother insisted on preparing home-cooked meals for me every Sunday. Some days she would sit on a chair in the kitchen because she was too tired to stand. I'd tell her not to worry about cooking for me, I would cook for her, but she always insisted. I asked her: "Is my cooking that bad?" She'd just laugh it off. The ultimate loving mother, she provided for her only child until she could no longer stand. I could only imagine the pain and heartache she must have felt when she had to close the door in my face while I was in active addiction.

The length of time my mother would be able to stand became minimal as she slowly became more and more dependent. My mother told me that she thought it was time to have hospice care initiated, and I moved in with her.

Hospice provided a hospital bed, a rollator walker, bedside commode, and outstanding nursing care. The bed was delivered and set up in the dining room, after I moved the table and chairs to the living room to make room for it. My mother could no longer ascend the stairs to her bedroom, but was still able to walk as far as the half bath, 15 feet from the dining room.

The hospice nurses were exceptionally caring and compassionate. We had paperwork we needed to complete and decisions to make. My mother opted for Meals On Wheels as back up to my cooking, and I was given power of attorney. Nursing staff asked if I wanted my mother to be resuscitated. I looked at her. She said no. The bare boned reality of the situation started to sink in, as the nurse said another nurse would come by to deactivate her pacemaker. I was instructed on the proper use of the contents of a large plastic baggie for my mother: various drugs that I had taken at one time or another to get high. The bag contained Ativan for anxiety, Valium, some tablets to increase saliva activity, fentanyl patches for extended pain relief, and Roxanol, a bottle of liquid morphine sulfate. I told the nurse that I was a recovered addict, and she asked if the liquid morphine bothered me. I told her: "Only if I use it."

As the days progressed, my mom spent more time in bed. I began sleeping in her bedroom upstairs with the door ajar, and gave her a bell to ring so I could hear her call if she needed me. I had been working at a skilled nursing facility for about five months, and I'd drive to my mom's during lunch to make sure she was okay and to heat up her lunch. I made sure everything she needed was within arms' reach before returning to work. After work I drove straight home, made sure she had dinner when she was hungry, and then went to a 12 step meeting most evenings for a couple of hours. I also trained with Grandmaster Sikes on Tuesdays and Thursdays. The combination of going to meetings and training helped me cope mentally and emotionally with the gradual decline of my mother's health and independence.

One early morning I heard my mother screaming for me. I ran downstairs to find her in the bathroom. "I can't get up from the toilet," she said. By this time her body had become bloated with edema in her legs and her trunk. Water pills kept her going back and forth to the bathroom. I tried to help her stand but she couldn't. She kept apologizing, but I told her it would be okay; I would have to carry her. I said a silent prayer and lifted my mom from the toilet seat and carried her into the dining room. As I tried to sit her up on the hospital bed, I lost balance and fell on top of her. I made her laugh by asking: "Now, who's gonna carry me upstairs?!" *All the years she's carried me, in one way or another, now it's time to carry her.*

My mother could no longer walk to the bathroom, so I placed a new bedside commode next to her bed and told her to ring the bell when she needed help using it. God knew exactly what He was doing when I was guided to be a physical therapist assistant. I had plenty of experience assisting patients transfer to commodes; the time had come to help my mother. I was humbled.

The bell I had given her was getting a workout, as she rang it all hours of the evening. I'd come downstairs and help her transfer to the commode where she would sit for hours. She said that she didn't want me to have to keep running downstairs in the middle of the night and that I needed to sleep so I could work in the morning. Just like my mother; always concerned for others. Selfless.

I applied for FMLA (Family Medical Leave Act) so that I could be at home to take care of my mother. I was given up to eight weeks off from work without pay with a guarantee to return to employment when I was able. My mother rarely slept at night and neither did I. Every morning I made oatmeal for her — she could eat some oatmeal! I wrapped her legs with Ace bandages and elevated them to decrease the fluid in her extremities. I made sure she had taken the appropriate medication and then I'd try to get an hour or so of sleep until lunch. About 6 a.m. one morning I heard the bell ringing frantically. I ran downstairs and my mother screamed: "I've been ringing and ringing for hours. I had to go to the bathroom and I think I wet myself!" She was embarrassed. We saw her independence slipping away. I said: "I think it's time to start wearing the adult diapers." I hated hearing those words come out of my mouth. I helped my mother clean up and change into dry pajamas. After hesitating at first, she conceded to wearing Depends.

I tried to make a meeting every night of the week. If I was unable to make an evening meeting I would attend a 15 minute meeting at noon downtown. The Wednesday night meeting that Tyrone S. and I started, New Direction, was a Godsend for me. I expressed all of my feelings and emotions and got feedback from others. It really helped. When I would feel like I was the only one going through this crisis I would be reminded that others had gone through similar situations. I used their experience to help me cope with my circumstances. By the close of the meeting I'd have new strength and be the best son that I could be for my mom.

Feelings of worthlessness and guilt sometimes hit me. Self-pity would rise up when I'd question God why other people had family members to help and I did not. To curb those feelings I reminded myself that had I still been drinking and drugging, I would have been unreliable and un-available to my mother when she needed me most. Being in active ad-diction when everything revolved around getting high, my mother's ill health and gradual demise would have been just the thing to get a free sympathy drink or rock on the house. I'd be off and running after I got the first one with no guarantees after that. I thanked God for the gift of sobriety bestowed upon me. Without it there was no way I could have helped my mother.

As time went on, my mother complained of painful spasms and anx-iety. I spoke with the hospice nurse about it and she suggested I give her some Valium. My mother didn't like taking anything that made her feel "out of control." It reminded me of why I was mentally and physically different from non addicts. When I took a mood or mind altering substance, I felt *in control,* not out of it. It does something for me and not to me. I gave my mother a 5mg Valium, and it calmed her anxiety for a short time, but she was in distress again a few hours later. I called the hospice nurse again and she said to try Ativan. I waited until later that evening, gave her half a pill and my mother slept well. She slept so well that she wouldn't wake up the next morning, noon or evening! When my mother did finally awaken she wasn't herself. The hospice nurse came over to check on her. She was slurring her words and seemed to be exhibiting some left sided weakness. I thought she may have had a stroke. Slowly she came around to her old self by the following evening. It scared the piss out of me! I truly thought she was on the way out. Once she came around she told me that was the best sleep she'd had in a long time! I told her that she would never make a good addict, and she asked why. "Because you can't hold your dope!" I said.

My mother experienced more discomfort as days passed. I wrapped and elevated her legs daily to decrease the swelling. She'd have leg spasms and worsening pain in her sides. At one time the edema had reached the trunk of her body. This made her very uncomfortable and compromised her breathing. I asked her if she wanted to try some of the morphine for pain and she agreed to. I made sure to give her only a teaspoon full remembering her sensitivity to drugs. It appeared to have some success with pain abatement, mostly because it knocked her out.

Staying in contact with a sponsor and support group is invaluable in times of turmoil as well as in times of peace. I learned not to isolate myself in times of emotional upheaval; I had to step out on faith. There were times when there was no one to hug or ease the intense pain of a loved one slowly leaving this world. I had to learn to trust in a God of my understanding. I didn't want my mom to die of course, I wanted her to be okay. I learned that in life, my wants are just that: wants. How selfish to insist my mother remain in pain daily for my self-centered needs.

My sleep schedule was upside down. I found myself trying to catch hour naps when possible, listening for her bell. Early one morning, the bell rang just as I was starting to fall asleep. I got up immediately and went to her. She needed me to transfer her to the bedside commode.

"This is wearing you down, isn't it?' she asked, noticing my obvious fatigue. I nodded.

"I'll be okay. I just need a little sleep." I said.

"I think it's time we check into finding someplace for me where I can have 24 hour help." I wanted to say no but my body relented. Had my mom not suggested a skilled nursing facility I would have continued to help her until I dropped, and she knew that. I reluctantly began the search for a facility. The first place I called had a bed available and was located less than 10 minutes away. I toured the facility and agreed to move my mother there. Within the week a couple of nurses arrived in a transport van, and they transferred my mother from the hospital bed in our dining room, onto a gurney, and then into the ambulette. As they took my mother through the front door I thought, *This will most likely be the last time my mom will see her home.* It was.

My mother moved into the area of the facility that handled hospice care. She had a private room and a color TV. "What more could you ask for?" she asked while settling into her new surroundings. She was examined by a doctor and was friendly with the nursing staff and the STNAs (state tested nursing assistants). I spent most days and early evenings with her the first week she was there, before deciding to go back to work. The staff at the facility was excellent and I trusted them. They were able to assist in healing a bedsore she had, and my mother began to flourish in hospice! She was taken off all of her heart and high blood pressure meds, and started feeling better for awhile. Every day after work I went to see her, a blessing that I lived so close. We watched the news together, then I would run home to fix something to eat, and head back to visit for awhile before hitting a meeting. I was permitted 24 hour access to visit, so I always returned after meetings to say goodnight.

Although my mother started to feel better, it did not last long. She was confused at times and could not figure out how to use the phone. It was easier to visit rather than call because if she answered the phone, it was usually upside down.

July 27, 2007 was my mom's 80th birthday, and I found out how many good friends she had. A close friend and co-worker of hers, Estelle, organized a birthday party. She and all of my mother's co-workers had known me since I was a child. My mother also had traveling and Tai Chi companions, four or five women she hung out with prior to her illness called The Cobbler Posse because they were all blueberry cobbler fans!

The party was held in a community room down the hall, complete with balloons, cake, ice cream, and presents. The Cobbler Posse was there, about eight of her co-workers, my youngest daughter, my close friend and sponsee Tyrone S. and his wife, Lisa, attended. My mother wore continuous oxygen and was getting progressively weaker. It appeared that she was having a difficult time staying at the party, but she refused to go back to her room when I asked. My youngest daughter, nine or 10 years old, spent most of her time in my mom's room playing with the controls of the hospital bed, watching TV, and making occasional visits to the party room to pick up some cake. Just like the feeling I had that my mother would never see her home again, I think we knew this would be her last birthday.

My mother spent more days in bed, and refused outdoor activities. She sometimes asked: "When is this thing going to come to an end?" She was tired of hanging around. I suggested that she get out of her room more, and shared with her what I had learned in 12 step meetings. The best way to release self-pity was to get outside of yourself. I told her that she could be influential to other hospice patients by encouraging them to enjoy their time and the people around them, and if nothing else, to be kind. Being a positive example would be of more value than being a miserable, self-centered old poot. My mother laughed and said: "When I grow up I want to be just like you!" I was surprised by my own advice, as well. It hadn't been that long since I was the miserable, self-centered old poot. I asked the nursing staff to get my mother out of bed and into her wheelchair daily; not only would it help her self-esteem but would also aid in digestion and breathing.

My mother started going outside to the courtyard patio in her wheelchair with me regularly, watching the birds and squirrels. Sometimes we talked but mostly we just sat next to each other silently. I had already made verbal and financial amends to my mother prior to hospitalization. But, sitting there in silence reminded me that I still had a lot more to tell her. How do I tell someone who always had my back how much they mean to me? How do I thank her for giving birth to me, taking care of me when I had chicken pocks, always standing up for me even when she was criticized for doing so? How do I tell her I love her for never giving up on me? We sat there daily, me on a bench and she in her chair, listening to the hiss of the oxygen flowing through the tube leading to her nose.

One season moved into the next as we watched the leaves change color and fall to the ground. We talked about Halloween costumes she made for me when I was a kid, and her joy watching her two granddaughters dance in the basement, trying to hold her attention. "Mam'mom watch this, watch this!" She'd give them her undivided attention and tell them how talented they were. I re-lived the past 51 years of my life with her in remembrance and gratitude. When it became too cold to sit outside we retreated to the warmth of the dayroom to watch the snow fall outside in the courtyard. We were not only mother and son, but became close friends.

Both of my daughters flew to Cleveland from South Carolina for Thanksgiving 2007. My oldest had not seen her grandmother for awhile and it upset her to see my mother so frail, and in a skilled nursing facility. She sat next to my mother on the hospital bed, holding hands. "Are you okay Mam'mom?" My mom said yes and inquired about what was going on in my daughter's life. Meanwhile, my youngest rolled up and down the halls in my mother's wheelchair dodging nurses, and an occasional patient. I felt energized having them there. That was my family all together again. It was a bittersweet occasion.

After the holiday, my daughters returned to South Carolina, and shortly after their leaving, my mother went back to spending more time in bed. She became bloated with edema and had to be medicated for pain. One day she went into a very deep sleep, and the nursing staff told me to prepare for the inevitable. I took a couple of days off from work and stayed at her bedside. My boss and co-workers were very understanding and supported me throughout my frequent absences. Her breathing was more labored and erratic, and I watched her heartbeat pulsate through the carotid artery on the right side of her neck: throbbing, stopping and starting again. I stayed in her room with her all night holding her hand and thanking her for all she had done for me and my family over the years. I said goodbye, whispering in her ear: "You can leave now. I'll be alright." Tears flowed freely from my eyes. The morning nurse came in to check my mother's vitals, while I left the room to get coffee. I stood outside the facility for some fresh air to revitalize me, and said a prayer, "Thy will be done." I walked slowly back to her room in time to see the nurse come out with a perplexed look on her face.

"You're not going to believe this!" she said. I went into my mother's room.

"Good morning," Mom said, barely audible. I gave her a kiss on her forehead.

"Welcome back!" I said.

CHAPTER TWENTY-FIVE

Testing Sobriety

I STARTED NOTICING an occasional sharp pain running down the back of my right leg. It gradually became worse and radiated down the front of my lower leg and into my foot. At times I could barely stand. I went to my primary doctor and he scheduled me for an MRI. The results concluded that there was an abscess in my lower back which put pressure on a nerve and caused the pain down my leg. My doctor prescribed Tylenol with codeine for pain. I told him that I couldn't take narcotics because I was a recovered addict. He said that I had legitimate pain and I needed it for relief. I told him my addiction didn't know the difference between legal and illegal drugs, and he would have to find something non narcotic to give me. He prescribed Neurontin; a muscle relaxer, Flexeril; and Motrin 800s. I couldn't take the muscle relaxer because it became to difficult for me to get up in the morning for work. The combination of Neurontin and Motrin masked the pain long enough to get through almost an entire day of work before it returned.

I was referred to a surgeon, and he said that he'd have to remove the lamina from my lumbar spine in order to access and excise the abscess. I'd be in the hospital for at least four days and off from work for at least six weeks, remaining in bed for the majority of that time. He asked if I had anyone — family, brothers, sisters — to help with my convalescence, and I said no. In that case, he said, I would most likely have to stay in a rehab facility. My brain raced trying to figure it out. *How am I supposed to get through this? I need to be available to my mother. I have to work. I can't do this!* I told my sponsor what was going on, and he suggested that I pray on it, and get another opinion. By chance, I mentioned my dilemma to a close friend, and she said that she knew of an older surgeon who was known for his talented surgical skills. I took the x-rays and computer disc with my MRI images to him. He looked at them and said he could remove the abscess without cutting away bone. It would be an outpatient procedure, and recovery time would be approximately two weeks at home. I almost kissed him! The surgery was scheduled for December 23, 2007.

MY MOTHER was not the same after her near death experience, much weaker and confused, and received morphine more frequently. One day, I walked into the facility and sensed something different. The nurses were not as talkative to me, the nursing assistant gave me a condescending glance, and the resident pastor said he needed to talk with me immediately. I went into my mother's room to greet her. She looked worried.

"Are you alright?" she asked.

"Other than my leg hurting, I'm fine. Why, what's up?"

"It sounded like you were in pain last night. You called out all night long!" she said. I was confused. I had visited my mother the night before but left around 9 p.m. because she had gone to sleep. Just then the pastor tugged at my arm, and guided me out to the common sitting room.

"Have a seat," he said firmly. "Your mother says you've been using drugs!" I thought my mom had told him that I was in a 12 step fellowship.

"Yes, the last time was a little more than eight years ago."

"No, last night!" He explained how my mother was telling everyone in the facility that I had started using drugs again and she was so worried about me. *Oh my God!* I looked him square in the eye.

"I've been clean for eight years and the last thing on my mind is picking up again!"

"Well your mother seems to think you are!"

"She's the one who's wasted with all the morphine she's getting!"

I rushed back into my mother's room, and had never seen her look so out of sorts, flustered and confused. She had always been on point and focused her entire life, but the progression of her illness was evident. Rather than stand at the foot of her bed and scream my allegiance to sobriety, I quietly and patiently assured her that her suspicions were unfounded. I had learned early in recovery that there would be times when we'd be accused of doing things that weren't true. Rather than defend ourselves with belligerent denial of the accusation, we should listen and respond without fanfare. "To thine own self be true." Once I finally was able to accept myself, live honestly without deception, and keep my side of the street clean, untruths didn't have the same effect on me as they did in my using days. During active addiction, I would get so pissed off at people accusing me of being wasted because I felt guilty when they saw the truth, despite my using Visine and attempting to act sober. It hurt when some-one knew I was lying and there was nothing I could do to convince them otherwise. I felt worthless. You can't move in truth when you're living a lie.

I talked to my mom for awhile, and learned that this was a deep fear of hers, as I had drilled it into her during my using days. It was almost like she was saying she was not going to die until she was sure I was alright. I spent more time with her the next few days so she could see nothing had changed in my dedication to living a sober life. Even after a couple days she gave me an occasional "remember, you can't fool me" look mothers worldwide have perfected.

Things slowly went back to normal. The nurses began talking to me, the nursing aide was cracking jokes and the pastor even blessed me! I remembered something Tyrone E. the monitor at Orca said: "You can't get clean for anyone else but you." It made sense. Had I gotten clean just to have my mother respect me then when she accused me of using I may have picked up out of self-pity because my reason for staying clean was gone. I'd learned that the benefits I received in sobriety were a by-product of living a spiritual way of life. I don't try to change others for my comfort these days, and if I slip back into the habit of trying to, I'm reminded why it doesn't work. It's a full time job making the world run the way I want it to! Once I change, my perception of the world changes. One day my uncle (my mother's brother) called the hospital room, and I answered the phone.

"David...your mother told me you've been using drugs!" he said. *Oh*

God! Grant me the serenity....

On the eve of my back surgery, I was a little antsy because I didn't know what to expect. I always wanted to be prepared for events because it gave me control over situations. In reality, I have no control over anything but my own actions. I can plan for a certain outcome but there's always the possibility that the outcome will not match my plan. If I take the action and put the results in the hands of my higher power, it is called faith; knowing that things will turn out the way they're supposed to, not necessarily the way I want them to. To quote Tyrone E.: "If it was supposed to be any other way then it would be."

A co-worker picked me up from home early the morning of the surgery. She was in a 12 step fellowship too, and passed along some encouraging words on the way to the hospital. I thanked her for the ride and she said she would keep me in prayer, which helped me walk through the hospital doors. A nurse checked my driver's license to make sure they didn't cut into the wrong person, and asked if I was allergic to anything.

"Narcotics," I said.

"What's the problem with narcotics, Mr. Smeltz?"

"There is no problem as long as I have more!" She didn't get it. I told her I was a recovered addict.

"I'm sorry to hear that."

"I don't use anymore; please be sure to let the doctor know." When she left the room, I took off my clothes and put on a backless hospital gown. I felt vulnerable and exposed with my butt hanging out. I started to repeat silent prayers as they wheeled me into the operating room. I was told to roll over onto my side with my butt facing the nurses! I wasn't liking this shit. The doctor came in, and upon seeing his smile and relaxed demeanor some of my anxiety eased. He drew a circle on my lower back, put a mask on me, and injected something into the PICC line that the nurse had applied. I was instructed to count to ten. I said: "One..."

The next thing I knew I woke up in the recovery room. Now that was some good dope! That instant coma shit...would've loved to have that when I was full of cocaine, listening to the damn birds remind me that I'd been up all night. The phone rang. An attendant said an old lady was on the phone who wanted to know if I was alright. My mother had her nursing assistant hunt me down and find the phone number to the recovery room! That took some effort; my mother really loved me.

The nurse brought some pills to me. I asked what they were and she said Tylenol #4 with codeine. I repeated: "I'm allergic to narcotics." The doctor came in and suggested that I take them. I would start feeling the pain, he said, as the surgery had been more difficult than he'd expected. He highly recommended that I take them. I scanned my memory for any information I had read or heard in recovery about a situation like this. I flashed back to a line in the Basic Text: "There are times, however, such as in cases of health problems involving surgery and/or extreme physical injury, when medication may be valid. This does not constitute a license to use" (*Narcotics Anonymous,* p. 98). And: "In this program of total abstinence, however, we need to feel no guilt after having taken a minimum amount of medication prescribed by an informed professional for extreme pain" (*Narcotics Anonymous,* p. 99).

I took the medication.

My close friend and sponsee, Tyrone S., was waiting for me to be released. I was given a prescription for Demerol, and I thought *It doesn't seem to matter how many times I tell these people I'm an addict!* I left with the prescription and not much thought about filling it. I was still a little spacey when Tyrone picked me up. I told him I had a script for Demerol, and he asked if I wanted to fill it. I said I should be able to handle the pain with Tylenol. He had been given a prescription for narcotics after his esophagus was ruptured by surgeons during a biopsy, and he said he was glad to have them available because he was in a great deal pain after discharge. He explained that I might miss having them later that evening when the Tylenol and anesthesia wore off. I asked him to drive by CVS so we could have it filled. The prescription was for 60 pills but the pharmacist said they had only 47. I told him I would probably take only a few so 47 was fine. Tyrone dropped me off at home, and I left a message at the nursing facility for my mother, letting her know that I was home and would come to see her in the next day or two.

A girlfriend that I was having an on and off relationship with called to see how I was doing. She said she wanted to come over to take care of me, and I was all in for some pampering. When she came over, she said she was sleeping with someone else. The timing for her honesty sucked. I screamed at her and told her to leave. I was feeling angry, so I decided to take a Demerol, to stop any pain that might pop up. How was that for addictive thinking? Sounded good to me. I wanted to dull unpleasant emotions, and was setting myself up by using rationalization and justification.

I began to build up resentment directed at my ex-girlfriend and whoever she was seeing. Self-pity popped up along with some self-created back pain that required medication so I took another tablet. The "normal" person would concede to the fact that there was no more pain so the medication was working. The addict (me) was wondering why he wasn't feeling anything. In order to feel something, I took another tab. I realized suddenly that it was probably not a good idea. I experienced old feelings of guilt, shame and remorse. Guilt: I was beginning to abuse my medication. Shame: I was in recovery and I knew better. Remorse: the guilt of ingesting that crap. I did *not* want to wind up doing heroin and smoking crack again, and brought my thoughts back to how things were before I got clean: shivering, snot running down my face, the uncontrollable urge to use even when I didn't want to. I was a slave to the drug and I remembered what it took to get clean. I lost my family and their respect; lived in a house with 16 men with as many personalities; tried to stay put and not run out to use; sleepless nights and tears, frazzled nerves; extreme loneliness; feelings of abandonment and suicide.

The moment of truth. I lay on my bed with the bottle of Demerol in my hand wanting to take another one and not wanting to take another one. There was a battle between good and evil going on in my head!

"God, please help me." I had come face to face with being powerless over drugs again. The only power greater than Demerol is God. I got on my knees and began to pray just as I had done at Orca House and every morning since. I asked God to help me make the right decision. I was on my knees for awhile. I stood up, picked up the bottle of Demerol and flushed the remaining pills down the toilet. There was most definitely a power greater than me working that evening.

Early that morning and the next day I felt dope sick just like I had used heroin. I now had a firm resolution not to use anything no matter how shitty I felt. This almost fatal incident thrust me into an even deeper desire to stay clean and sober. I cannot take the first pill, the first hit, the first drink or the first of any mood or mind altering substance without it setting off the phenomenon of craving which guarantees my inability to stop. I knew this before but I had to have it branded onto my psyche so I would never forget!

I was terrified that I would pick up again if I didn't stay on top of my recovery and start living by spiritual principles. I wanted to blame someone for this (typical addict behavior) but I realized that no one put a gun to my head or shoved the pills down my throat. I thought about blaming Tyrone. I called him later in the week and told him what had happened. We realized there was one key component missing from my experience with prescription meds: Tyrone's wife had control of his pills and gave them to him accordingly. I, on the other hand, had total control over dispensing my meds. It was like giving an inmate the keys to the prison and telling him not to open his cell!

MY MOTHER became weaker as days passed. Although she attempted to assist, she was dependent on others to move and transfer her. We spent a bittersweet New Year's Eve together in her room. I couldn't help but think that this may be our last holiday together. I continued to go to 12 step meetings to share what I was feeling, and my support group became my larger family as my biological family (aunt, uncle and cousin) were not able to be there, and my daughters were ten hours away in South Carolina.

We continued spending quality time together, and every now and then I'd bring a friend or two by to visit. She enjoyed seeing my friends, and I think she wanted to make sure I was hanging out with good people. She wanted *me* to be okay until the end. I told Mom I had been reunited with an old party buddy, who had been sober much longer than I, and the interesting fact that we were both sober. My mom wanted to meet her, so I brought my friend to visit and she perked up, putting on her formal/hostess persona. She told my friend that she had heard good things about her and was happy about our sobriety. My mother then recited the Lord's Prayer in Latin! This was a first for me. She learned it in high school, and I told her I was impressed. She smiled.

Around mid January my mother's breathing became increasingly labored. Fluid had started entering her lungs more frequently, her extremities were cold to the touch, and she was sleeping more often. The nurses said that her organs were beginning to shut down. I had worked with patients before that required suction so I asked nursing to bring in a machine to help clear her airways so that she could rest more comfortably. I watched the nurses use the machine on my mom as she occasionally gasped for air. I held her hand as she struggled to breathe. She squeezed my hand with all of her strength as I tried to comfort her. I felt helpless. I repeated silent prayers for my mother's comfort and for God's will.

My mom went into a deep sleep. The nurses told me that it was getting close for her departure. I stayed with her, watching as her breathing became erratic. She'd take deep breaths and then exhale. It seemed like hours before she'd inhale again, and I'd hang onto every breath. I looked intently at the veins in my mother's neck as they displayed her heartbeat pounding forcefully with intermittent pauses. After two days of staying by her side I told the nurse that I was going home to take a shower and eat and I'd be back in a bit. I said: "Be sure to call if there are any changes."

I went to my mom's condo and passed out on the bed for a bit. I woke up early evening, showered, ate something and went back to hospice. When I arrived they were suctioning my mother. I told my mom I was there and held her hand again. Her eyebrows raised a little as if acknowledging my presence. The nursing staff had been giving her eye droppers full of morphine by mouth, she wasn't able to swallow, hoping that some would get into her system. I didn't want her to be in any pain.

The nurse with her that evening was from Jamaica, the same one who helped heal her bedsore when she arrived months earlier. She was very nice and she and my mother had a good rapport. She was extremely caring and comforting to my mother as were all the nursing staff and health aides. They all became my temporary family because they comforted me, as well.

My mother jolted violently, and began coughing up a light brownish milky fluid from her lungs. She struggled to breathe. The nurse said that this had been happening all evening and would subside after a few minutes. I had surrendered to the reality of the situation days earlier. It was time for the inevitable. I held my mother's hand and stroked her forehead with the other, the entire time telling her how much I loved her. She began resting peacefully.

The nurse asked if I'd said everything that I wanted to her, and I said I had.

"Did you tell her that it's alright to leave, that you're going to be alright?" she asked. "She's not going to leave without your consent."
The nurse left the room and I whispered in my mom's ear that I loved her and that I'd be okay. Then, the most difficult thing I ever had to say.

"It's time for you to go, Mom. It's alright. Thank you for being my mother. I love you so very much. You can leave now." I asked the nurse to come back in.

"You know, I don't think she wants you to see her go." She said I should go home to get some rest and she'd call me if I was needed. It didn't really register what she was saying, but I agreed to go home and told her I'd be back in the morning. It was midnight February 2, 2008.

I went back to the condo and climbed into bed with my clothes on. It seemed as though I had only been asleep for a few minutes when the phone rang. The nurse said my mother just passed away. I looked at the clock, it was around 1 a.m. She asked if I was alright. I was numb. She was with my mother when she took her last breath and I thanked her. I said I was on my way. She told me to drive carefully and be safe. It felt as though time had stopped. My mother was dead.

CHAPTER TWENTY-SIX

Love and Loss

MOM'S DOOR, which was usually open, was closed when I arrived at hospice. I walked into her room and saw her laying on the bed with her eyes closed. I went over to her and put my hand on her forehead which I had done many times before. Her skin was still warm to the touch. Although it was her body before me, it felt as if I was observing an inanimate shell of what had once been her. *This isn't my mom!* Her lifeforce had gone. Even when she was ill there had always been an energy emanating from her that was now noticeably missing.

I stayed for approximately one half hour. We had said our goodbyes to one another during the months leading up to this day, and I had made living amends to her by staying clean and helping others. I'd come to know that nothing was permanent; not everyone would like or agree with me; those that supported me today may turn their backs tomorrow; and nothing in the world will always be the way I want it. The most important thing for me was to go to bed clean and sober.

As I walked from my mother's room I glanced back once more and said goodbye. I felt alone physically, but supported spiritually. When I was using I was alone physically and spiritually. The combination would bring thoughts of hopelessness and suicide. Having the spiritual component brings clarity to any situation. In my opinion, there is an ever present and loving energy which promotes life. It is all inclusive and operates whether we realize it or not. We don't have to believe in it. I do believe that we cut ourselves off from realizing this source when we become our main priority. For me, it was only by surrender of the power which I thought I had, was I able to allow a new power in. No matter how much willpower I had, I couldn't put down the bottle and the stem (pipe). It was not until I stopped fighting, surrendered and asked for help that I was given the "real" power. This was a Truth from my experience.

I stood outside of the hospice facility and called my best friend and sponsee, Tyrone S., and told him what had happened. He asked me if I was alright and did I need him to come by. I told him that everything was okay and I planned to call my sponsor next. My sponsor also asked if I was okay, and said he was on his way if I needed him. I told him that I was fine.

"There's a 12 step convention this weekend in Beachwood. They're having marathon meetings," he said. Message received loud and clear. I drove the 15 minutes to the convention at 2:30 a.m. on Sunday morning, within hours of my mother passing away. I fell into the role of chairperson of the 12 step meeting. Exactly where I was supposed to be.

My mother was someone who planned things well in advance. She always seemed to be on top of everything. I never heard a swear word or a complaint leave her lips. My grandmother, however, introduced me to the phrase, "God damn it to hell!" and a few more profane utterances at an early age.

My mom had orchestrated her own homegoing. She gave me a choice of three dresses she could wear at the viewing, and she let me decide which pieces of jewelry. I had a list of people to contact after her demise, and she had prepaid the majority of the funeral expenses. She instructed me to give the silk Tai Chi jacket that she purchased in China to her Tai Chi instructor, and she requested that the class perform at her funeral.

Her boldest request had to do with her cremation. She wanted me to sneak the cremated remains of my dog, Loki, in with her ashes during the interment! Loki was an all white shepherd/wolf mixed-breed that I found foraging for food one day after work in Cleveland. I put him in my car and took him to my mother and grandmother's home. He was about a year old and malnourished. He worked his way into my grandmother's heart by jumping onto the stove and eating a whole corned beef in three bites! My mother and grandmother took care of him when I was on the road with the band. Loki was very protective of them. I knew they'd be safe when I was out of town.

My two daughters flew up from South Carolina for the funeral. My friend and pastor, a red sash master student of Grandmaster Sikes, performed the ceremony and gave the eulogy. My mother's closest friends, The Cobbler Posse, and friends from work, 12 step members, my aunt, uncle, cousin, sponsor, Tyrone S., a few of my friends that knew my mother, the lead guitarist from I-Tal, and my mom's Tai Chi group attended.

The Tai Chi class performed, and my oldest daughter shared loving words about her "Mam'mom." My uncle spoke reminiscently of his sister and the pastor concluded the ceremony. The urn with my mom's ashes was passed to me, I then passed them to my youngest daughter and then to my oldest who walked them to the site of interment. There was no way I could sneak my dog's ashes into the vault without being noticed. I apologized to my mother under my breath; Loki's ashes remain in my closet. Perhaps awaiting someone to sneak them in with me when I'm cremated. Sounds like a job for my daughters!

Something in me changed after the funeral. The day that I had feared and dreaded while in active addiction had come and gone. I knew now that there was no reason to pick up a drug or a drink under any circumstance.

I continued to sponsor guys, go to meetings, talk to my support group and increased my martial arts training with Grandmaster Sikes, even during my mother's illness. Once, I told him that my mother was having pain and muscle spasms in her legs, and he made a concoction of Chinese herbs and rubbing alcohol that his teacher, Master Reeders, had taught him to make called "Dit Da Jow." He said it was for bruising and muscle pain and we used it to keep the swelling down after training. Grandmaster introduced me to a style of meditation he performed. In order to know when my opponent is about move I needed to have a quiet mind, and the only way to get that was through meditation. He taught me two ways that had worked for him. One was to sit cross legged facing a burning candle and keep my eyes fixed on the flame to improve concentration. He also told me to draw a picture of a bulls-eye, the kind used for target practice. He said to focus my attention on the center of the bulls-eye for 15-20 minutes. If neither candle nor bulls-eye were available then I should keep my focus on the Dantian (Tan T'ian). The Dantian or "Field of Cinnabar," a Daoist term referring to a center of energy located approximately two inches below the navel and inside the lower abdomen. The location roughly corresponds to the center of mass of a person standing in a natural posture, hence, it is often referred to as the "center of being."

Grandmaster also shared information about The Five Elemental Energies: Wood, Fire, Earth, Metal, and Water and how they related to the changing of the seasons and internal organs of the body, as there is much more to martial arts than fighting. There's an internal and spiritual component as well as physical. Grandmaster talked about self cultivation and of developing "Chi," the natural energy or lifeforce of the body. I focused on cultivating my internal strength/spirit. It is that same spirit that strengthened and carried me through the loss of people I loved, and past the stuff that I thought I deserved/were afraid I wouldn't get/were afraid to lose. Grandmaster was kind and inspirational. He, my sponsor, and Tyrone S. were the closest family that I had after the passing of my mother in February, 2008. Actually, they were the closest to real family that I'd ever had.

In June, 2008 Grandmaster was admitted to the Veterans Administrations Hospital. I had trained with him at his home prior to the week of his admission. Along with many of his students from all over the country, I visited him when it was clear that his prognosis was not favorable. My friend and teacher Grandmaster Arthur Sikes died July 3, 2008. He taught martial arts for more than forty years and was a loving and giving spirit. I'm a firm believer that all people and things are put into our paths for our edification. Each one teaches one. Our teachers live on if we share the lessons we've learned from them with others.

In October of the same year, my longtime friend, affectionately known as "Music Barry," passed away. He owned a local music store for more than 20 years, and was instrumental (no pun intended) in furnishing equipment for I-Tal, and almost every other band/musician in Northeast Ohio, along with major touring acts. Barry was a talented musician, sound man, and lighting expert. I bought my brand new 1978 Les Paul Custom from him on a payment plan along with our PA system in the '70s. Later, I sold most of my equipment back to him to buy crack. Much of what I sold to him he didn't need or want, but bought it because he knew I was fiending. He refused, however, to buy back the Les Paul no matter how much I begged.

On summer days, he would open the front door of his music store, sit down at a Hammond B3 organ, and would start wailing on it while puffing a big 'ol funky smelling cigar and kicking the Leslie speakers up all the way. The front windows would rattle and people at the bus stop in front of the store would peek in, unable to enter because of all the energy he was putting out. We did our share of partying together too. Unfortunately, he succumbed to the party in 2008 after intermittent lengths of sobriety. *But for the grace of God.* I had firsthand knowledge of impermanence and the never ending cycle of life and death; in order to *get* through pain you gotta *go* through pain. According to Tyrone E.: "When you're walking through hell, don't stop!"

On the last page of Grandmaster Sikes' eulogy was the following poem:

Do Not Stand at My Grave and Weep

Do not stand at my grave and weep,
I am not there; I do not sleep.
I am a thousand winds that blow,
I am the diamond glints on the snow,
I am the sunlight on ripened grain,
I am the gentle autumn rain.
When you awaken in the morning's hush
I am the swift uplifting rush
Of quiet birds in circled flight.
I am the soft stars that shine at night.
Do not stand at my grave and cry,
I am not there; I did not die.

– *Mary Elizabeth Frye (1932)*

PART IV
CHAPTER TWENTY-SEVEN

A New Direction

IN 2009, a young woman that I worked with at a geriatric facility texted me: "I think I like you." This probably wouldn't have meant much at any other time but I had been trying to talk to this lady for a long while. She worked on the third floor of the facility and I would visit her first thing in the morning, as she had a caring and professional vibe about her. We'd talk and shared some laughs at work, and she was a source of comfort and support when my mother was ill. I was fresh out of an on/off two year relationship with an active alcoholic which was tumultuous to say the least.

I called her to ask if the text was a mistake or if her kids were playing around with the phone, but she said she was shy. We started dating, and I met her son and daughter, both nice kids. I really became attached, though, to her four-year-old daughter and she became attached to me as well. In time, she would hug me and call me daddy, something I enjoyed hearing from my own daughters, albeit infrequently. We began talking over the phone on a daily basis, and never ran out of things to talk about. Not long after we started dating, she left the facility where we both worked.

One day I received a bouquet of roses at work. No one had ever sent roses to me, and I was hooked! I told myself that I would never marry again after experiencing such a painful and emotional divorce, but I was so taken by this woman that I asked her to marry me. She accepted. I introduced her to my sponsor and support group members. My best friend Tyrone S. loved her and said that I needed a good woman like her to keep me in line. I even told my aunt and uncle about the upcoming marriage, and they were happy for us too. My daughters met her and it seemed that I would be able to enjoy having a family again. I vowed that I would not make the same mistakes I had made in my first marriage; drugs and alcohol would definitely be excluded from this relationship as well as my emotional immaturity, so I thought. She didn't drink or smoke which made it even more perfect. Things went well for a year or so and then we began to have disagreements. Her children came over with her to spend the fourth of July with me and my daughter, who was in town for her summer visit. I took the kids to the pool and enjoyed helping her four-year-old learn to swim (mostly float) in the pool while their mother slept. It had been a long day and we didn't go to see fireworks that evening.

Later that night, she called to ask if I had placed an advertisement on a local dating service website. I had put up a personal ad before we started dating but neglected to take it down. There wasn't a picture, and it basically listed my interests and hometown. I had forgotten all about it and said that I'd put it up along time ago. She got pissed, and I got pissed. I was so angry that it never crossed my mind to ask her why she was studying profiles on a dating site! I had grown "little" in my sobriety. I prided myself on being able to handle situations without raising my voice but that went out the window, as I resorted to my old ways of conflict management: yelling.

"For someone who is so into spiritual stuff you sure can be an ass-hole!" she spat.

I agreed with her, and started taking inventory of myself and remembering what my sponsor once told me: I can always remove myself from the situation. So I did. But I learned that avoidance is not a solution either! For days I wouldn't call, waiting for her to call me. She did a couple of times and we'd patch things up and get back together. We went through this dance of death a few times and then she told me that she wasn't going to call back anymore. I didn't believe her, just like I didn't believe my wife when she told me she wanted a divorce. I was wrong on both counts. My fiancée called some five months later, and I was excited to hear from her but not about what she had to say. She said she was moving on and want-ed all pictures that I had of her because she wanted to start her new rela-tionship with a clean slate. My emotions vacillated between heartbroken and pissed. It was the same feeling as when my wife and daughters left me: rejected and abandoned. A feeling of gloom and loneliness covered me and I wanted the pain to go away. I threw the phone across the room and said a few not so nice words. I picked it up from the corner, put the battery back in, powered it up and called her back.

"Sorry, I just threw my phone across the room. Can we meet somewhere to talk about this?"

"No!" she snapped. BAM! My phone hit the wall again! I knew this wasn't good. I recalled what I'd read in our literature: Whenever I am upset about someone, something or some situation the problem lies within me.

I had to sit long enough to inventory myself. This time I let the cell phone sit in the corner while I looked at the part I played in the situation. I knew I had to make amends to her for my actions, and I wanted to save the relationship if I could. My motivation for making amends already housed an ulterior motive: to get back together. I sat and inventoried further. *No matter her reaction to my apology, I will be civil in speech and respectful.*

I called back from the home phone and told her I wanted to apologize for my reaction. She said she still didn't want to see me anymore. I gritted my teeth and reminded myself of my promise to remain civil throughout the conversation no matter what. Earlier in our relationship I had given her a turquoise ring that my mother wore all the time, and I had given her an engagement ring too. I asked her for my mother's ring and she said she thought someone had taken it. I then asked her to return the engagement ring and she said she'd lost it. BAM! The landline hit the wall.

At this point, I learned that I was not where I thought I was in my sobriety. I beat myself up for failing to handle situations more maturely, and realized that in order to grow in sobriety, I had to confront situations so that I could learn how to work through them without freaking out. When I tried to control situations and outcomes, I set myself up for disappointment every time. I'd always wanted the security in knowing how things would turn out. If I twisted this and said that or did this or did that then the results would be to my liking. Guess what? Not everything nor everyone marches to my direction. This was a tough lesson that I had to be reminded of occasionally.

Tyrone S. and I were still facilitating the Wednesday meeting we had started in 2007. Along with the meeting we would share our experience, strength and hope with the men and women in detox at The Harbor Light facility every Sunday. Tyrone and I were close, and strengthened our recovery together by sharing our experiences. In 2009, I introduced the idea to Ty about starting a non profit transitional housing program. After living at Orca for 104 days, then going to further treatment at the PASS program for eight months, I knew the value of a safe living environment for men and women leaving treatment and heading back out into the world without support. Living in a place with recovery-based teaching was invaluable to form a solid foundation to live a clean and sober life. Tyrone said he was onboard with it.

"Good, 'cause you're the treasurer!" I said. Tyrone had been treasurer of our homegroup for years and I trusted him with my life. I would set up a non profit corporation requiring additional board members. I told my sponsor, Ron H. what we were trying to do and he was up for it as well. I explained to Ron and Ty that I wanted martial arts to be included in the curriculum, and shared how it helped me tremendously with focus, connection with mind and body, and exercise. That brought my thoughts to my teacher, Master Rob, who was my martial arts instructor since the passing of Grandmaster Arthur Sikes. Master Rob was also a pastor, and brought with him a spiritual component to our mission. We needed one more person to complete the board of directors. An old party buddy of mine had been sober for more than 20 years, and I made a stop at a meeting she was facilitating. We caught up on old times. She was the friend I took to visit my mother in hospice, as it was a blessing to see recovery working in her life. I asked Meg E. to join the board.

The original name we selected for the non profit organization was The Foundation. After conducting a search of non profit organizations, we discovered that the name was already in use. I thought about being clean and sober in a house, which came together as Clean House. We did a search and there wasn't a Clean House, Inc. Later, we found many "clean house" agencies for profit, and we needed to distinguish ourselves from the companies that provide that service. I began to think of an acronym for CLEAN. I sat in meditation for a bit with the acronym as a point of intention. The answer came rather quickly: "Changed Lives Empowered And New." I shared our non profit name with a friend.

"Did you mean to do that?" he asked.

"Do what?"

"Have the initials of the organization spell CHI?"

"No, I didn't." In Chinese culture, chi is an active principle forming part of any living thing, and is frequently translated as "natural energy," "life force" or "energy flow." Chi is the central underlying principle in traditional Chinese medicine and martial arts. The literal translation of "chi" is "breath," "air," or "gas." Clean House, Inc. is where we hope to resuscitate and breathe life into recovering addicts and alcoholics.

In 2011, I noticed Tyrone was losing weight. He had never been large in stature but it was obvious he was slimming down. Also, every so often Ty would call and say he wasn't feeling well and that he wouldn't be at our Wednesday meeting to facilitate. When my mother was ill and I couldn't make it, Tyrone was always at our meeting making coffee, passing out Honey Buns (which he always purchased), and facilitating the meeting. This was a special meeting to us because it was for people with emotional and mental problems as well as drugs and alcohol, and it was the first meeting we started together. It was our baby. There were residents in the facility that came weekly and we had become close. One evening during the meeting Tyrone left abruptly saying he'd be back in a minute. I continued the meeting to the end and Ty had not returned. I found him outside sprawled across the front seat of his truck with the door open. I asked if he was okay and he told me that every now and then he would get a jittery nervous feeling like he was out of control of his body. He was also having tremendous back pain, making it difficult for him to sit comfortably for extended times. I could tell that it scared him, and it scared me too. He scheduled an an appointment with his doctor.

That same year, my sponsor's sponsor (my grandsponsor) committed suicide. He had approximately 18 years sober, and no one knew the exact circumstances surrounding his death. What was known was that he stopped going to meetings and alienated himself from the fellowship. He and my sponsor were as close as Tyrone and me. When I had a year sober my grandsponsor escorted me on my first spiritual retreat, and he was an excellent example of recovery in action for me. He was the first to tell me that God speaks through people, a concept I believed in whole heartedly. But in order to hear the message I have to listen. My prejudices and judgments can cut me off from something I need to hear or see from another human being. I'll always remember feeling God's presence as my sponsor, grandsponsor and I got on our knees and prayed on a hilltop together at a retreat in Pennsylvania. I also remember a lady walking by us as we concluded our prayer.

"Now that's something we need to see more of," she said.

"What's that?" I asked.

"Three men praying together!"

God speaks through people.

I continued to go to meetings, incorporate the 12 steps into my life and sponsor other guys when asked. One of the most important tools for staying clean and sober is to work with another addict/alcoholic. The idea is to get out of myself and to stop focusing on my perceived problems. Once I have a working knowledge of the steps it's my purpose and duty to carry the message to the sick and suffering drunk and/or addict. "Practical experience shows that nothing will so much insure immunity from drinking as intensive work with other alcoholics. It works when other activities fail." (Chapter 7: "Working With Others," *Alcoholics Anonymous*). "By this time, most of us realize that the only way that we can keep what was given to us is by sharing this new gift of life with the still-suffering addict. This is our best insurance against relapse to the torturous existence of using. We call it carrying the message..." *(Narcotics Anonymous,* pps. 48-49). We also carry the message by facilitating meetings and sharing in detox centers. I believe this was what helped advance Tyrone and me into recovery and kept us there.

Tyrone brought the topic of using pain medications to our next Wednesday meeting. After my Demerol experience, I was adamant about not using narcotics for anything. I told him that we sometimes create more pain than there really is, and that Tylenol should be sufficient for pain. Tyrone got pissed off! I'd never seen him so angry.

"What if that shit don't work?!" he spat. He then said that his oncologist told him that cancer had started spreading into his bones, and especially his back. He didn't want to use narcotics for pain but he had to because the pain was becoming intolerable. Tyrone was also concerned that this would change his sobriety date. I think he was also scared that he might start to abuse the medication as well. I changed my tune right away, and couldn't imagine how much pain he had been in all that time.

"By all means, take the pills!" I said. Ty calmed down a little and said that his wife would have control of the medication. "Good 'cause we both know that a monkey can't sell peanuts!" I said and we laughed. We had heard this from Tyrone E. when we were clients at Orca House.

Tyrone and I had attended Founders Day in Akron, Ohio for 11 years together. June, 2012 was no different except that Tyrone wasn't feeling well. Usually we had a sponsee or two along with us but this year it was just us. We sat in the bleachers together in the stadium. There was a sobriety countdown and we both stood up at eleven years and hugged one another as we had done every year.

Ty looked at me. "It's been a long trip together, hasn't it?"

"Yep, and many more ahead!" I said. Tyrone smiled. I knew that he had forced himself to go to Founders Day. He was usually there with me for the entire day, but this time he made it only to the big meeting on Saturday night. He looked tired, and we'd often sit down to rest for a few minutes before continuing the walk to and from the stadium. After the meeting, we walked to our cars and talked about our commitment to sobriety. I gave Ty a hug and he turned to walk slowly to his car. I watched him and wondered if this would be our last Founders Day together.

Occasionally, Tyrone missed our Monday homegroup meetings, but he'd always call to let me know if he couldn't be there. Early July, 2012, Tyrone showed up at our homegroup. Although we didn't know it then, this would be his last time attending. We had a meeting with a topic to discuss. I immediately put a question to the floor.

"How do you help your best friend when he's really sick and you feel powerless to help?" At that point tears poured out of my eyes, as I had said something aloud that I had only thought to myself. The reality of the situation sank in. Tyrone looked at me with a typical humorous smirk.

"I assume you're talking about me." He said then proceeded to talk about having faith and trusting the process. Every few words he would clear his throat. His voice sounded weak but his words were to the point, as Ty never sugarcoated anything. He talked about having faith in God and knowing that God had a plan for us. We had always talked about putting ourselves in our higher power's hands since we met at Orca. He looked at me from across the table.

"Don't count me out yet, Smeltz...we never know what can happen. Did you ever think you would get sober?" he asked.

"No, never."

"See what I mean?" My tears continued and it was difficult to speak. This was never in the plan, as Tyrone and I were supposed to continue walking arm and arm through recovery together as we had been doing for the past eleven years. He was supposed to be part of Clean House, Inc.

and take guys through their 12 steps like we had done numerous times together. We were going to help other addicts and alcoholics like we had been helped, and give back what was so freely given to us. My sponsor reiterated what Ty had spoken: "Trust in a power greater than yourself." I had no other choice but to take that advice. I had to; I was powerless.

We took meetings to Tyrone's house, which he greatly appreciated. His wife would give him his meds while we had our discussion. All of our homegroup members attended including my friend and board member, Meg. Our newest board members, Laura and Jennifer were present and a part of the family as well. We were able to bring three 12 step meetings to Tyrone's home in mid July to early August of 2012.

Tyrone and I had talked about making a short promotional video for Clean House. We attempted to tape on several occasions, but Ty was either too ill or just not feeling up to it. Mid July, Tyrone went into the hospital to have his lymph nodes removed from the right side of his throat. After the procedure, his health deteriorated rapidly. He stayed in the hospital for a couple of days after the surgery, and on July 15, I received a voicemail from him.

"I'm out of the hospital and at the house. Now maybe I can get some rest. When you get a chance give me a call."

I called Ty later that day and he told me that he thought it was time to do the video for Clean House. A few days later, Laura, Jennifer and I met at Tyrone's house to tape the interview. Laura and Jen had been helping and supporting Tyrone's wife, Lisa, during this time as well. As I sat on the couch with Ty I felt the brotherly bond that I had always felt with him; especially when we started to talk about recovery, as it was the bond that brought us together. It is what saved both of our lives and opened our eyes to a new way of living. As he spoke, I had a flashback to the many times he and I shared at the detox center with other suffering addicts. His voice, now wavering and interrupted by an occasional clearing of his throat, still carried a strong message of recovery. We were in our element:

Recovery! We talked for nearly an hour while Jennifer posed questions and Laura videotaped. It was a jovial atmosphere and Ty and I shared our thoughts, hopes and experiences in recovery. I prayed this would not be our last time doing this together. I could see that Tyrone was getting tired, so I suggested that we stop. Tyrone said: "Yep, we can continue this another day."

A couple of days later, Tyrone's wife called to tell me that Tyrone was having difficulty breathing and his back pain was worsening. She told me that Tyrone had requested to be taken to the hospital, so I knew he must have been catching hell to request that. Tyrone's wife called again the next day and suggested I might want to come see him.

"He's not doing so well," she told me. Those words were a shock coming from his wife, as she and Ty had always been so positive and supportive of one another. I knew it was serious. I called our homegroup members and Clean House board members and relayed Lisa's message to them. I arrived at the hospital to see Ty in bed with his eyes closed and breathing heavily. The length of time between inhalation and exhalation would shorten and lengthen.

When I walked in Lisa spoke in Ty's ear: "Dave's here, Tyrone." He didn't respond verbally but Lisa pointed to his heart monitor and his heart rate appeared to increase after she said that. "He knows you're here," she said. I went over to the bed, hugged him and held his hand. I began to cry as I released Tyrone's hand and hugged my friend, Meg.

I left the hospital that evening and was struck by the familiar hammer of powerlessness over the situation. The power that I do have in any situation is that of my personal Higher Power where I've learned to put my trust. Personal experience and not hearsay has and continues to enforce my belief. I can be sure that if I'm bent out of shape and stressing or worried over something, then I've left my Higher Power out of the equation. And it was not until I'd reestablished a conscious contact with this power am I able to find some peace with a situation. Trusting in this power doesn't mean the outcome will necessarily be what I want it to be. It does mean, however, that the resulting answer will be the correct one no matter what I want or think should happen. And I have to be okay with that. It's called acceptance.

I returned to visit Tyrone the next day with my girlfriend after work. Tyrone's son, daughters and other family members were there. They had been there since the previous night and most of the following day. We entered his room and stood next to his bed. I hugged him, just like we had always greeted one another. The intervals between his inhalation and exhalation were longer than the night before. I stood there with my girlfriend and Tyrone's son watching his labored breathing. Ty's son started telling stories about his dad, perhaps to console himself. He spoke respectfully and candidly, and said his dad was no angel, but was always a man of his word. None of us were angels in active addiction but recovery taught us not to *talk* about it but to *be* about it. In other words, it taught us to be responsible.

Tyrone's son had seen both Ty's active addiction and his sobriety. It's not easy for family to forgive or forget how we were when we were caught up in the grips of addiction. Tyrone and I learned that we can't change the past but we don't have to live in it either. Some family members may never forgive us. Once we make sober amends and restitution to those we've hurt, we can continue our living amends to them by remaining clean and sober. We no longer allow people to hold what we did in the past over our heads: we walk this earth free men. Tyrone's son had forgiven his father and was now feeling the pain of not knowing whether his father realized it or not.

I met Tyrone's youngest daughter for the first time in his hospital room. Tyrone and I talked about our children all the time when we were in treatment together, as his youngest daughter was a year older than mine. When we talked about them at Orca they were three and four years old, and now they were teenagers. I said her dad talked about her all of the time at Orca, and loved her very much. I then asked Tyrone's son to keep me updated on his father's condition. I kissed Tyrone on his forehead and left the hospital.

Once my girlfriend and I reached the lobby, I looked at my watch. I told her that I needed to get to a meeting, and I knew there was one on Broadview Road; the same meeting that Tyrone and I would go to when I lived on the westside. It was also the meeting that I went into loaded years ago before I surrendered. A lot of memories came flooding in as I sat and tried to listen to the speaker. I kept thinking about my friend back at the hospital, and the countless hours we spent walking the road of recovery together. Sharing things that only the two of us would ever know and learning how to live life on life's terms through trial and error.

My closest and dearest friend was leaving me and my self-centeredness kicked in. Some guy tried to hit on my girlfriend at the table where we were sitting. After yelling at this dude, and disrupting the meeting, we left. I apologized to my girlfriend and she suggested we go back to the hospital. The problem was that I needed to let go of Tyrone, and tell him goodbye, but I didn't want to let go of someone who meant so much to me. I was also afraid that I'd be alone in my recovery from then on.

We went back to the hospital. I said a quick "Thy will be done" and walked to Tyrone's bedside. I bent over and whispered in his ear and told him how much he meant to me and that he was the only brother that I had ever had. I was being selfish wanting him to stay around so that it would make me feel better. I told him that I was letting go and giving him to a power greater than either of us. I told him, goodbye.

On my way to work the next morning my cell phone rang. I knew before answering it. Laura was on the phone, as she and Jennifer had been staying with Tyrone's wife Lisa, offering support. Laura told me that Tyrone had passed away. It was the morning of August 10, 2012.

Tyrone's funeral was held Wednesday, August 15, and my sponsor and I, and others, spoke words of remembrance. The funeral home was packed with Ty's friends and family, Clarence Fluker, and a few guys we sponsored. People from the fellowship showed up in full force as well. As I looked in his casket I saw that his life force had left his body, just as it had my mother's body five years earlier. I still saw the image of my true brother and comrade. As the preacher spoke, I glanced at my watch, 7 p.m., the same day and time that our Wednesday meeting usually started. A week after Tyrone was unable to facilitate our Wednesday meeting the facility told me that they would be closing. They began the process of moving all of the clients to other facilities that by the time of Ty's funeral, the meeting we started together at Cleveland Rehab was no longer. I couldn't help but think of the impermanence of all things. When Ty left, the meeting followed.

Thinking about the name we had given it, New Direction, brought it all together for me. At every ending there is a beginning. It was the beginning of a new direction without my best friend and brother, Tyrone. Everything changes; nothing stays the same. I've learned that I'm the one who suffers when I try to keep things as they were rather than accept things as they are. Holding onto that which gives me pleasure and avoiding the unpleasant has me either chasing or running away from things. As Tyrone E. used to say: "Live in the solution and not the problem."

There are no real problems; just issues that come up that need to be addressed. I heard someone say: "Issues are like tissues; as soon as you pull one out another follows right behind it." I figured that I could either cry into a tissue or blow my nose into it! The only real obstacle is me. I get in my own way at times. The more I realize that the world does its thing with or without my consent of what should happen, the more I'm able to adjust my course accordingly through perceived obstacles which appear before me. Is it easy? No. Neither was getting clean and sober. Is it gratifying? Yes! And so is staying clean and sober. Just for today.

EPILOGUE

Clean House, Inc.

IN LATE 2009, I decided to put an idea to paper that had repeatedly nudged me from time to time throughout my sobriety. The idea was to start a sober living environment that would be safe and supportive to addicts and alcoholics in their beginning months of recovery. I wanted the residents to be able to focus on learning to live clean and sober without making food and shelter an immediate priority, as it would be provided free of charge. Their center of attention could then be devoted to building a solid foundation in sobriety prior to finding employment, rather than getting a job first and trying not to spend the entire first paycheck on mind and mood altering substances. If there's no solid defense against the first one then the job won't last very long anyway. In my opinion, we have to practice fortifying our sobriety by living and following the program of recovery suggested in the 12 steps. I'm not arguing the fact that there may be other avenues of recovery from alcohol and drugs. I am only promoting what has worked for me and continues to work for countless others. I can only attest to my personal experience with the 12 steps of recovery.

This living and learning environment would be conducted as a not for profit organization, and will house only six to ten men. The objective is to serve as a schoolhouse as opposed to a warehouse. The individual sponsoring of men is fairly impossible in overcrowded conditions. I believe that a smaller number of men will benefit greatly through camaraderie geared toward achieving a shared goal of recovery.

| 203

I attended a 12 step meeting one evening and the speaker spoke about three things we should consider doing as recovering members:

1) Trust God

2) Help Others and...

3) CLEAN HOUSE!

Clean House! That's it! We had a name, but needed to add something to distinguish us from Mighty Maids. I sat in meditation for a short time and an acronym for CLEAN came from nowhere: Changed Lives Empowered And New. Plus, the initials for Clean House, Inc. support our body, mind and spiritual connection. CHI is the lifeforce within our bodies, also referred to as "Spirit."

In addition to founding board members Pastor Robert Edmonds, Tyrone Saunders, Ron Harris, and Meg Elliott, we had two additional board members for a brief time, Denys Morgan and Brian Kilgallon. Both added valuable contributions and support to Clean House, Inc. and we thank them wholeheartedly for their dedication to our mission. Following the departure of Denys and Brian, Laura Coiley Dietrich and Jennifer Coiley were elected Board members, and my brother in recovery, Tyrone, passed away shortly thereafter.

To provide recovering men with spiritual and mental tools needed for continuing personal growth and prevention of relapse. Clean House strives to promote consistent and contented sobriety by addressing all three elements of addiction; the body, mind, and spirit.

– CHI Mission Statement

ADDICTION is a three-fold dis-ease which affects us spiritually, mentally and physically. When all three aspects of addiction are addressed we can recover. Abstaining from the use of all mood and mind altering substances is primary before attempting to resolve these three areas of importance. For this reason, Clean House will only accept men that test negative for drugs and alcohol via initial and ongoing urinalyses, and have completed a minimum of 30 days inpatient treatment. He must also have general knowledge of the disease concept of addiction. Clean House has a zero tolerance policy for anyone testing positive for alcohol and/or drug use.

All men will be introduced and instructed in the 12 steps as outlined in the Big Book of *Alcoholics Anonymous*. Initial sponsoring of men will be provided by staff until each man has a working knowledge of the program of recovery. The sponsored man may either continue with the staff sponsor or obtain a co-sponsor after successful application and demonstration of the principles within the 12 steps. The 12 steps help us rectify our difficulties with a Higher Power (steps 1-3), self (steps 4-7), and others (steps 8 and 9). Daily application of steps 10 (self assessment), 11 (spiritual alignment), and 12 (service to others) allow us to grow daily in our recovery process. Clean House is not affiliated with any religious organization or denomination. We do, however, support all residents in their subjective comprehension and attainment of a power greater than themselves.

Mental focus and concentration are severely impeded by excessive drug and alcohol abuse. In response to this problem Clean House will offer daily meditation and mindfulness instruction. I have personally found meditation to be of great value in learning to watch my thoughts rather than reacting to them. Learning to sit in silence and observing the present moment is most rewarding. Coming into recovery my thoughts were all over the place. The more I focused and identified with my thoughts the more they multiplied. The more they multiplied the more lost in thought I'd become until I would completely lose contact with the present moment. Any minor distraction, someone coughing, flicking a lighter, car horns blaring, commanded my attention. I'd be all over the place. Thoughts of the past of the future or both would take me out of the now. In my opinion, there is no palpable past or future. The past no longer exists and the future has not yet arrived. All there is is this moment. And in this moment our future begins and our past surrenders its grip; unless we willfully hold on to it. If I want a conscious contact with a power greater than myself it has to be in this moment. For me, that's where all possibilities and grace reside. In this moment. While in active addiction I never could sit still long enough to be in the moment. I was always in expectation of the next thing to come. Plus, I might miss something somewhere if I sat still too long! I have now learned to sit with myself. When I take the practice of being mindful throughout the day I'm more relaxed and less reactive to events. I'm more able to respond than react.

CLEAN HOUSE will address the physical malady by practicing martial arts as an outlet for releasing emotional stress and frustration. Learning to recognize and release negative energy in a healthy and safe way is a necessity of monumental importance for living contently in sobriety. Residents will learn the basics of self-defense and will be instructed in Kata forms which can then be accessed whenever needed as a method of moving meditation. Moving meditation (Kata forms) can be implemented as an important recovery tool to redirect anger and promote serenity. We have lost the right to use drugs and alcohol to medicate our problems. Now, we can learn to meditate our problems.

Daily 12 step meetings will be held at Clean House and will be open to the public as well as our martial arts classes and mindfulness training. A number of Yoga instructors have expressed interest in teaching at our facility once we're up and running. We are looking forward to offering "Urban" Yoga classes for our residents and the community. We plan to be a proactive resource hub with access to computer classes and GED preparation for our residents. Our plan is to assist our men in obtaining a firm foundation in sobriety and guidance toward successful community reintegration in association with local merchants and vendors.

CLEAN HOUSE, INC. purchased a building located at 11910 Buckeye Road in Cleveland, Ohio in November 2013. We signed a contract to purchase the property the previous April. We were not allowed possession until its previous owners satisfied a lien. At the time of signing the property had been vandalized. Two furnaces and electrical wiring from the basement had been stolen. A vacant property security firm removed all windows and entry doors and replaced them with grates to secure the building. We patiently waited through eight monthly extensions until the lien was resolved and we were able to take ownership. During the eight months of waiting, the building was vandalized again. The cabinets and sinks in all three kitchens had been stolen, along with toilets and fixtures, and the second floor (remaining) furnace. Vandals also tore into walls looking for copper piping. We were granted a slight reduction in purchase price on the property but have more to replace and repair than we had originally prepared for. Our goal for 2014 is to have all windows and doors installed, and electrical work completed.

Clean House exists through donations, and we are in the process of researching available grants. We will open a "gently used" clothing store in one of the storefronts to assist in sustainability. All proceeds from this book will go to Clean House as well. We accept donations at our website www.cleanhouseinc.org.

We also accept donations at information tables while participating in various local events. Refer to our website for specific locations and dates. Please consider a contribution to Clean House, Inc. We are a 501(c)3 tax exempt non profit organization. If you have any questions or wish to volunteer to help, please contact us at cleanhouse.smeltz0@gmail.com.

You don't have to be in recovery to support those who are.

Since the real purpose of meditation is to increase our capacity to help others, taking time each day to meditate is not selfish. We have to manage our time and energy in such a way that we can be of maximum benefit to others, and to do this we need time alone to recover our strength, collect our thoughts, and see things in perspective. – Geshe Kelsang Gyatso

I AM FORTUNATE and most blessed to have lived two lives in one lifetime. One impaired by drugs, alcohol, and defective thinking; and a second, liberated by divine intervention with resultant clarity of mind (for the most part). One could not have happened without the other and for both I am truly grateful.

I have watched some friends and acquaintances pat themselves on their backs while telling me stories about how they stopped drinking and drugging. They grin and tell me that they only smoke weed now and don't drink, or they only drink beer and not hard liquor, or they stopped doing coke and now only smoke herb. None have said they have stopped using all mood and mind altering substances entirely.

Most of these people are not full blown addicts but the remaining may be. The latter being on the installment plan until they get tired of trying not to use what they really want to use to get loaded. I can't count the times that I'd switch from one intoxicant to another trying to convince myself that one drug was less worse than the other. There are people who can use drugs and alcohol socially and successfully. I'm not one of them! When finally coming to the understanding that I am mentally and physically different from those that can use without penance and have mastered the ability to control their use, I could finally stop the ongoing war of attempting to use successfully and ultimately surrender to the inevitable: addiction.

THE PRESENT MOMENT turns into the next moment, which is actually still the present moment. It's not very difficult to stay clean and sober just for this moment. If you tell me I have to stay clean for the rest of my life...

then we have a problem! You hear in recovery fellowship: "It's hard by the yard but a cinch by the inch!" which means that I can certainly do in a moment what I would have trouble doing in a year. It's the "One Day At A Time" thing broken down into being fully present in this moment. And how does one learn to be present to this moment? I can only speak on what has and continues to work for me. Meditation has been a most beneficial tool in learning to watch my thoughts and allow them to pass. I practice sitting meditation twice daily; in the morning and evening before going to bed. I sit for at least 30 minutes at a time, sometimes less depending upon time constraints. When in a rush to get to work I'll stop and make time for at least five minutes to center myself before leaving. It makes a tremendous difference for me. I now understand that when I grab onto or attach myself to a thought then that thought grows into another thought and then another. Soon I've got these scenarios going on in my head: things that happened when I was five years old; to thoughts of where I'll be buried when I die or if I should be cremated; to what am I going to eat after work and so on!

The past is gone and future is not here. So all of these thoughts are actually about things that don't exist. I've completely taken myself out of the now where everything is possible. I drive daily as part of my work, and it's easy to get lost in trivial bullshit. When I am mindful of my thoughts and center my attention to my breath, I'm able to attend to life as it is happening at this moment. Daily practice in martial arts assists in present moment awareness by focusing concentration while being mindful of each technique and movement within each form (Kata). Of course, we all have goals and plans for the future. I just don't dwell on them. I have faith that if I'm facing the right direction and taking positive and constructive actions the goals will draw me toward them rather than stressing out trying to chase after them.

"In order to keep it; you have to give it away." I have to be available to share what was freely given to me. That means I sponsor new people in recovery by taking them through the steps, by making sure they have a thorough working knowledge of them, and are able to apply them to their life. Going through this process not only helps the newcomer but the sponsor as well. It reinforces my sobriety and encourages me to be of service. After all, I can't very well share a working knowledge of the steps if I'm not living them myself. The best way to get me out of self is by working with another, which has gotten me out of self-pity mode many a time. Plus, there's great joy in watching someone transform from a hopeless dope fiend into a dopeless hope fiend! Another, if not the most important, tool in my sobriety tool box is a God of my understanding.

Religion is belief in someone else's experience. Spirituality is having your own experience. – Deepak Chopra

SOMEONE ONCE TOLD ME "Religion is for people trying to stay out of hell; spirituality is for those whom have already been there." I totally identified with the statement. My conception of God at the time I surrendered was that of some old white guy with a white beard, throwing thunderbolts down from the clouds. And for all the bad things I had done in my life, I was guaranteed a trip to hell. I had heard about "The wrath of God," "An eye for an eye," and I had seen what God did to the Israelites when Moses (Charlton Heston) threw the 10 Commandments to the ground and they exploded. Remind me never to worship a golden calf! All these images and more assured me that a spiteful and jealous God would surely be pissed at my scandalous ass. I had heard of a God of love but it seemed to me that He only loved you if you followed every one of His rules. And if this were the case, I was on my own!

When I was introduced to some 12 step reading material, the word "God" kept popping up. I knew I was going to have trouble from the get-go due to my beliefs about God. Fortunately, my sponsor told me to find a higher power or God of MY understanding. I had already proven to myself that heroin, crack and Cuervo were a much higher power than me. So, I had to find a power more powerful than they. My first higher power consisted of my peer group at Orca House. We all, pretty much, surrendered to Orca House. I slowly realized that all the 12 step people at the meetings we attended were an even greater power because they knew how to stay sober and we didn't. A Group Of Drunks (G.O.D.). And then my sponsor became my higher power for awhile. In my first year of sobriety, I attended a spiritual retreat, and was told that God speaks through people. My conception of God has grown into a personal relationship with a loving and forgiving power in my life. I have found a variety of teachings that promote spiritual principles to live by. What works for me may not work for others. I do, however, believe I must acknowledge one thing for certain: I no longer run the show!

There comes a day when you realise turning the page is the best feeling in the world, because you realise there's so much more to the book than the page you were stuck on. – Unknown

WHILE IN ACTIVE ADDICTION, no one could have convinced me that this world and all of its inhabitants weren't put here just to annoy me. My priority in active addiction was to make sure I had enough dope and alcohol to get me through the night and day. The kicker is that there was never enough dope and alcohol to get me through the day or evening. I always worried about running out. I hated the police, the dope boy, my ex-wife, the courts, anyone with a smile on his face, and all those suckers going to work every morning while I was still geeked from the night before. I felt worthless, hopeless, unwanted, and unloved. I couldn't stay still at a job long enough to get a full two week paycheck because I was obsessed with using. In those last days my life revolved around getting more and using more. I never want to be in that situation again. I will always remember that time in my life. I truly believe that I had to be stripped of all that I valued in order to learn to love myself instead of loving what I possessed or held dear to my heart. The "things" in my life once gave me validation as a man. Now, I realize that a man's worth is not found in his possessions but in how he treats himself and others. Today I can be alright with life the way it is. Only by actually being homeless I learned that when I can't pay a bill or two at their due date I don't have to freak out. At least I can stay at a job without fiending for dope all day. I know that I will get a paycheck. I sometimes jump to the most negative conclusions, so I have to be diligent in monitoring my thoughts and beliefs daily. The very worse case scenario is that I will become homeless (from a couple of unpaid bills!). I put down what money I can on them at the time but still my mind will tell me that I'm irresponsible and a loser. My thinking can be my worst enemy if I allow it to be. The reality is that I've been homeless and it wasn't the end of the world. Learning how to live without anything instilled my faith and trust in a Power that strengthens me in all situations. No matter if I don't hear from my daughters, someone passes away, I'm behind in bills, broken promises, my girlfriend leaves me for another man, or whatever the case...I don't have to pick up a drink or a drug!

Unless we base our sense of identity upon the truth of who we are, it is impossible to attain true happiness. – Brenda Shoshanna

EVERYONE LIVES his or her own individual truth. Although, most people's truths are based on someone else's beliefs. This isn't a bad thing. In the beginning of my sober journey my truth was based on others' abilities to stay clean and sober. I'm consistently growing in this process and as a result coming face to face with a person I've never met before: Me. The more I get to know myself, the more I see outer influences and conditions that make up David Smeltz: the reggae guy, the physical therapist assistant, the martial arts dude, the addict, the alcoholic, the guy that looks somewhat like President Obama.... All labels and perceptions from other people which I can either attach to or acknowledge and let go of. The more I identify with various personas the more I live someone else's truth. I believe people either like or dislike their perceptions of who they think we are and not our actual beingness. There's a certain freedom in not defining "me." That which I think I know only limits me. It's in the not knowing which opens the door to all possibilities.

MY HOPE is that my experience will help another out of darkness or at least plant a seed of hope. I'm not an authority on recovery and neither do I speak for any 12 step program. My "bottom" isn't necessarily your bottom, nor does my recovery have to be your recovery. We all have stories to tell. It is out of my deepest gratitude for sobriety that I share mine with you. My life has been positively changed, empowered, and made new. I am forever grateful.

David Smeltz
April 2014

JENNIFER COILEY is a writer, creative professional, and principal of Coy Lee Media, LLC. She contributed to David Smeltz's amazing story, **CLEAN:** **From Reggae to Recovery,** through editing, designing, and publishing. Ms. Coiley can be reached at coyleemedia@gmail.com or from her website, coylee.com.